All-Color
BASS
FISHING
Guide

Bill Herzog

All-Color
BASS
FISHING
Guide

Bill Herzog

Frank Amato

PORTLAND

Dedication

To Frank Amato, for his guidance and patience.

Acknowledgments

My thanks to Ron Soden, the Evergreen Bass Club of Washington state and the Bass Anglers Sportsmens Society for field and technical advice.

About the Author

Bill Herzog currently lives near Seattle, Washington, where he has lived most of his 35 years. Bill is also the author of *Spoon Fishing for Steelhead, Color Guide to Steelhead Drift Fishing, All-Color Bass Fishing Guide* and has a regular column appearing in *Salmon Trout Steelheader* magazine.

© **1995 Frank Amato Publications, Inc.**

Frank Amato Publications, Inc.
PO Box 82112
Portland, Oregon 97282
(503) 653-8108

All photographs taken by author except where noted.

Book design and layout: Tony Amato

Softbound ISBN: 1-57188-003-8
UPC: 0-66066-00193-1

Printed in HONG KONG

1   3   5   7   9   10   8   6   4   2

Contents

Unquestionably, since the 1890s, when James Henshall wrote the first comprehensive book on American bass fishing, *Book of the Black Bass* and James Heddon introduced artificial bass lures, bass have made indelible marks on American angling like no other species. Since the turn of the century, numbers of American anglers have grown exponentially with each passing decade. Post World War II saw the birth of spinning reels and monofilament lines, which caused a tremendous expansion in sportfishing with bass leading the way. The initial professional B.A.S.S. (Bass Anglers Sportsmens Society) tournaments in 1967 caused an explosion of new techniques, and with today's methods and advancements in tackle the nation's most popular game fish is targeted by more anglers than ever before.

Because there is such a great number of beginners learning about the sport of bass fishing, there will always be a need for basic "how-to" books. This need we will try to fill with this text. Admittedly, there are dozens of books available for the bass angler. However, most target experienced bass fishermen or deal exclusively with a specific technique. On the other hand, most beginning "how-to" books are much too general, omitting simple techniques and lack adequate information on types of lures. While this book deals with basic techniques and lures, it also focuses on bass habits and, most importantly, how to find bass regardless of which part of the country you may call home.

Chapter One gives you a general background of the two most popular species of bass: largemouth and smallmouth. You will read how to identify both species, their range and behavior. Chapter Two is the most important portion of the text: reading water. More so than lure choice, technique, etc., is knowing where to find bass under given situations. Thinking like a bass naturally increases your chance for hookups.

Chapter Two discusses how to locate bass under different temperature ranges, type of structure to look for, bass foods, where bass hold under degrees of water clarity and where to find them at different times of the year.

Chapter Three focuses on the three basic presentations for stillwater bass, ones that have little to do with any one type of lure but can be used in 90% of all lake/impoundment situations.

Chapter Four covers the most popular artificial bass lures and the most effective ways to fish them. It covers techniques, riggings and how to match lures to conditions. Chapter Five looks at the tools: rods, reels and lines. We'll see which rods, reel designs and space-age fishing lines will make your bass fishing easier and more effective than ever before. Finally, we will touch on bass fishing ethics and show the proper way to release fish.

All-Color Bass Fishing Guide does not include maps of popular waters, nor a listing of any "top 10" places to go. There are too many variables and opinions concerning criteria for "best" waters. Besides taking up too much space (a listing of best waters would require an additional book), the idea conveyed here is to take knowledge gained and apply it to your "top 10" waters so you may consistently catch bass.

Chapter 1

American Bass: Characteristics, Species and Distribution

Like all game fish, bass have seemingly "extra" wits about them, as they are tuned into their environment to a greater degree than other species of non-game fish. It's these heightened senses—smell, sharpness of eyesight and ability to hear or detect vibrations—that make them cagey adversaries.

The sense of smell is most important to a bass due to its rather poor eyesight. Because it is so important, it is the keenest of the three senses. Bass use sense of smell to locate food, locate a mate during spawning season and possibly to tell if a predator is in the area. In limited visibility situations, smell aids bass in finding prey. Studies show that bass that have been caught and released or have been stressed or injured give off a scent that alarms other bass. On several occasions divers have observed lures handled by fishermen after touching stressed bass have caused other bass in the area to totally ignore the lure or caused them to nervously move away. On the other hand, the scent given off by a wounded baitfish, such as a minnow or chub, can trigger a feeding stimulus.

Hearing, or more specifically, the bass' ability to detect vibrations, is as important as smell. Bass, like most game fish, "hear" with their lateral line and inner ears. Both play a different yet significant part. The inner ears are used by bass to first locate food, then the lateral line tells the bass which direction it came from. Bass locate foods and predators by wave frequency. A distressed minnow, for example, gives off erratic waves as would a pursuing predator. Even in murky water with almost no visibility, bass can zero in on a wounded baitfish and, luckily for anglers, any erratically moving plug, spinnerbait or worm.

While on the water, keep this ability to detect faint vibrations in mind. Shuffling around in tackle boxes, dropping beer bottles or other sudden movements can be detected quite easily by bass, especially in shallow water. Splashing oars and anchors dropped overboard alert every bass within a football field's radius. Even loud talking should be avoided. Stealth and quiet while on the water catch as many bass as the best lure for the conditions.

Least prominent but still important to bass is eyesight. Bass possess a tremendous range of vision, almost 360 degrees. They have a wide peripheral, can see almost straight down and up, nearly behind them and a full range in front. Even though bass have this unusual vision range, they are nearsighted and can only see clearly a few feet in front of them, even in ideal water clarity situations. They chiefly rely on smell and hearing (vibration) to locate food.

However, once prey-or lure-have been located, bass possess excellent close-up vision. This trait probably explains why a bass swiftly halts its attack inches from a lure when only moments before it was hurriedly moving to inhale it.

Bass do show a sensitivity to light, but direct sunlight does not affect their eyesight. During springtime, bass will lay in shallow water in bright sunlight for warmth, but generally they associate light with exposure to predators and stay under or next to cover.

Now let's take a closer look at the two most popular bass species in America.

Largemouth Bass
(Micropterus salmoides)

Largemouth bass.

When you talk bass fishing in America, you speak primarily of the largemouth. No other species of freshwater game fish is so widely available; all 48 states and Hawaii have thriving populations. Some of the best fishing for largemouth is south of the border in northern Mexico. However, it wasn't always that way. Before early stocking programs you could only find largemouth from Minnesota to Texas, east to Florida up to the Carolinas and up through Ohio and into the Great Lakes region. So well have bass adapted to western states that some of the biggest bass are no longer exclusive to warmer southern states; California now boasts some of the largest and fastest-growing fish in the country and many believe the next world record bass (currently a 22 pound, 4 ounce largemouth) will come from southern California.

Largemouth inhabit every conceivable type body of water you can imagine, from giant reservoirs to tiny farm ponds to tidal rivers and, except for high mountain lakes, everything in between. There is no general statement for habitat preference, as the largemouth is likely the most adaptable game fish. They are equally at home in a warm, shallow, murky-water farm pond as they are in a massive cold-water Columbia River reservoir.

The physical characteristics of the largemouth (also known as black bass) and its two subspecies, the spotted bass (*Micropterus punctulatus*) and the Florida bass (*Micropterus salmoides floridanus*), are easily identified with subtle differences. The spotted bass varies from the largemouth in that it has a more pronounced fork to the tail and sports a tooth on the tongue, which is absent on the largemouth. The Florida strain is different only in that it grows to a greater size, even though it is an actual largemouth. Coloring in all species of largemouth is generally the same: black back, dark green/black mottled sides, dark green to green/white bellies and a pronounced irregular black stripe down the lateral line. To give an average size for largemouth would be impossible due to the great variations in water temperature, type of diet and size of lake/impoundment they live in. A 5-year old largemouth living in a small, northwest

Washington lake may be full grown at 20 inches while one of the same age in a huge southern California impoundment may be 10 pounds.

Largemouth bass spawn during spring. After water temperature has risen to 62 degrees or above, they seek out fine gravel in shallow (2 to 4 feet deep) sheltered areas away from windward shores where they dig circular depressions (called "redds") and deposit their eggs. Largemouth spawn in shallow water so the sun's warmth may incubate the eggs.

Smallmouth Bass
(*Micropterus dolomieui*)

Smallmouth bass.

The smallmouth is a quicker, more determined fighter than its cousin, the largemouth. For this reason smallmouth are the author's favorite bass.

The smallmouth does have one advantage over its largemouth cousin, that being quality of fight. Any bass fanatic will tell you that "smallies" out-fight their kin by leaps and bounds, literally. In American freshwater game fishing circles, only steelhead and Atlantic salmon are held in higher praise when discussing difficulty to bring to hand.

There are two basic ways of identifying smallmouth from largemouth. One is by coloration, as smallmouth have dark vertical bars and markings while largemouth markings are horizontal along the lateral line. The most common body colors exhibited are a tan/brown with slight hints of orange. The second way to identify a smallie is to check the mandible bone on the base of the jaw. Notice where the end of the bone is in relation to the eye; if the bone does not extend past the eye, it's a smallmouth, as all mandibles on largemouth extend past the eye. Speaking of eyes, if the bass you are holding has a red eye, it's a smallmouth.

Originally found only in rivers draining into the Great Lakes and upper Mississippi, smallmouth have adapted to lakes and reservoirs in its original range and throughout the West. The giant impoundments of the Columbia River on the Washington/Oregon border are now regarded as some of the best smallmouth fisheries in the country due to impressive numbers of large fish. Unlike its relative the largemouth, smallmouth have a lower tolerance range of water temperatures. "Bronzebacks" cannot survive in water less than 36 degrees and no more than 80, which make it a prime candidate for impoundments that keep water temperatures cool and fairly stable throughout the year.

Smallmouth are on average more diminutive than largemouth, with an average size of 1 to 3 pounds. A 6 pounder is considered a trophy. Again, bass size is directly related to their environment, as a large, warm southern lake with plenty of feed produces bigger smallmouth than a tiny, cold northern facsimile. Smallmouth are gregarious, they love each other's company. Once you catch one smallie, you can assume that there are several to dozens of others close by.

Also spring spawners, smallmouth seek out leeward sides of lakes or wide, quiet stretches of river to build their nests once water temperatures rise to 65 degrees. Unlike largemouth, smallmouth tend to be a bit more haphazard where they build nests, as boulders and old stumps are as acceptable as fine gravel.

While a largemouth's feeding habits can be generalized into just about any available aquatic or terrestrial it can swallow, the smallmouth has a more predictable diet. It is estimated that over half of the smallmouth's diet consists of crayfish. Like their bigmouth cousin, smallmouth are still opportunistic feeders, but once you have located the majority of a crayfish population for a body of water, you can catch smallmouth.

Chapter 2

Reading Water:
Lakes and Reservoirs

To be a successful bass fisherman does not require that you spend thousands of dollars on state-of-the-art boats, electronics and tackle. Having these items certainly helps, but the truly skilled basser knows the most important tool is the ability to *read water*. To consistently find fish you must be able to go to any reservoir, lake or pond at most any time of year and apply the four variables: water temperature, structure, water clarity and available foods. Do it right and you can catch bass anywhere in their range.

Our main goal for this chapter is to help you find bass. When you put it all together and holding areas can be pinpointed, 90% of the work is done and it then boils down to proper choice of lures, which we will discuss later. This chapter concentrates on stillwaters, such as lakes and reservoirs. Rivers have been omitted, even though some of the best smallmouth fishing is in eastern rivers. Due to great numbers of plantings all over the country, the majority of bass fishing—for smallmouth and largemouth—is done in stillwaters. Lakes and reservoirs are more accessible and easier for beginners to read.

Make no mistake, there are more variables to finding bass than you can imagine, and there is no simple formula that applies to all waters. There are some facts to bass behavior that can be generalized, and for the sake of beginning bass anglers, we will stick to those basics.

Finding Bass By Temperature, Time of Year and Structure

While we touched briefly on preferred temperature ranges for both largemouth and smallmouth, we can now go into some greater detail. Bass, like all freshwater game fish, are cold-blooded creatures. This means their level of activity, primarily feeding and responsiveness to lures, is directly related to water temperature.

Bass can live in a water temperature variance from 34 degrees up to approximately 88 degrees without ill-effects. Prolonged exposure to temperatures under 33 and over 90, however, are lethal. Bass prefer a temperature range from 65 to 75 degrees, do best at temperatures up to 85 and display greater frequencies in feeding as temperatures climb from 70 degrees on up. Locating these preferred temperatures is a major key to finding bass.

Obviously, one of the most important items a bass angler must own is a quality water thermometer. Simply guessing where bass may be, perhaps just looking for struc-

ture or fishing the same area all the time because "they were there last week," has little merit. A thermometer tells you which section and depth of the lake/reservoir these ideal temperatures can be found, eliminating guesswork.

While it is difficult to generalize exactly where and when in stillwaters anglers may find bass, there are five time periods when bass show changes in behavior. Once you become familiar with these calendar periods you can adapt this table to your waters. These stages of bass behavior are important to recognize as they help determine which lures are most effective.

This pre-spawn largemouth was taken in 52 degree water on a spinnerbait.

Bass season begins each calendar year when fish move from deeper water to stage in spawning grounds. Bass move and become active when water temperatures climb above 53 degrees. This first period, pre-spawning, normally occurs during spring, although weather and water clarity play large roles. Sunny weather warms water faster, while cloudy, wet days may push this date back a bit. Clear lakes and reservoirs do not warm as fast as those that are off-colored or stained as dark water absorbs more heat. Prior to spawning bass tend to school and feed heavily. The pre-spawn period can produce some of the best fishing of the year. Watch weather patterns closely and check temperatures of your home waters to determine when the pre-spawn move initiates.

Once water temperatures have risen to 62 degrees and above the second period, the spawning stage, is under way. Bass are now in shallow water (2 to 10 feet) and are constructing nests, laying eggs or guarding fry. During the spawn bass tend to shut down and become unresponsive to lures. You know when this happens, as the great fishing you had just days before can suddenly shut down. All bass do not spawn in a certain body of water at the same time, so you may have to work a bit harder to find bass still in pre-spawn mode.

Keep in mind that all sections of a lake, except for perhaps ponds or tiny impoundments, do not warm up at the same time. There can be a variance of 5 or 6 degrees from one part of the lake to another. This is typical in reservoirs, as water flowing into the upper end keeps temperatures lower. Look for warmer water near dams or shallow inlets. Here you will find slightly warmer temperatures and the first active, aggressive bass of the season. In natural lakes and ponds the shallower water near shorelines is first to warm, and it is here in the shallows where you will find early season bass.

The third period, post spawn, is when bass can be the most difficult to catch. Females gravitate back to their deeper holding areas and cease feeding for several weeks making them difficult, if not impossible, to catch. Males are guarding nests and fry which makes them more vulnerable to any lure posing a threat to the young. After the spring spawn both males and females go through a resting and rejuvenating period. As water temperatures climb bass become progressively more responsive to lures.

The fourth period, summer peak, is the longest part of the bass season. By now both males and females have recovered from spawning and are established in their holding areas. Even though bass are at their peak of activity due to the season's warmest temperatures, food supplies are more abundant than at any other time. As a result what happens is the phenomenon anglers call "the bite", which means bass have become predictable as to time of day they will feed. This normally occurs during dawn and evening hours. There is one problem during this time: although bass are actively feeding, you must now compete with abundant natural foods for the bass' interest.

Weather patterns are the key to fishing success during the summer peak. Prolonged, searing hot weather can raise water temperatures above 80 degrees in smaller lakes and impoundments. Above 80 degrees, bass activity takes a plunge for the worst. Cold fronts—the arch enemy of all bass anglers—with rain and chilling winds can shut down fishing as if someone threw a switch. Look for stable weather during summer to ensure bass will be on the bite.

The last period, late summer/early fall, is next to pre-spawn as far as the best fishing time of the season. This period occurs just before lakes turn over. Nighttime temperatures become cool, almost cold, yet daytime highs may still be quite warm. Morning dew on lawns is a giveaway for this period. Bass sense oncoming colder weather and go on a major feeding binge. After lakes turn over and colder autumn weather drops water temperatures below 56 degrees, bass become lethargic and tough to entice.

Rock points, such as this one, are prime locations to find bass year-round.

Look for structure that creates hiding areas, such as overhanging or submerged tree limbs.

Now that you have an idea of what to expect during bass season you next have to recognize holding areas. Bass are structure oriented fish, anything that looks like it may hide a bass just might. Structure comes in many forms from weed beds to downed trees to rock points to old creek channels and so on. Bass use structure not only for shelter from predators and weather, but for hunting grounds and trapping and cornering prey.

Rock points are prime bass areas. Points provide shelter both for forage fish and bass. They cast shadows during bright days and act as a buffer from winds. Currents in lakes and reservoirs, as slight as they may be, swirl around these points creating a back-eddy behind leeward sides. These back-eddies collect plankton and aquatic insects which attract forage fish and bass that eat them. Points usually have one or two sides that drop sharply into deeper water. This affords bass with a sense of security, something important for all bass holding structure. Drop-offs from points are the in-between ground for shallow water feeding areas and deeper water escape routes from predators. Rock points with drop-offs can hold bass during an entire season, as variances in temperature can be found at changing depths along the drop-offs. Bass will find a depth along the rock point that best suits their ideal temperature range.

If you fish reservoirs an old map of the area before the dam was completed can be invaluable in finding structure. Bass love old creek channels—boulders, sharp banks or log jams make ideal cover. Look for these old channels near stream inlets. Not only are these shallower inlets the first areas in reservoirs to warm in spring, they usually have twice the cover and structure of the main channel. These maps can also show locations of humps or submerged islands. Like points, they attract aquatic feed as well as provide bass with a nearby escape to deep water sanctuaries.

When fishing these underwater spots use a marker buoy once the area is located. The inexpensive, hollow plastic H-shaped markers with the cord and weight wrapped around it are excellent work savers. Simply toss the marker buoy overboard over the spot and it will unravel itself until bottom is reached. Now you have a marker that shows you the approximate location of these holding areas without having to relocate them after you've drifted away.

Boat docks are favorite bass holding structure, they are custom-made predator blockades and great shade makers. Docks are also usually built on shorelines of lakes and reservoirs, which are the richest portions as far as insect or weed growth. In shallow lakes (less than 20 feet deep) the best cover, especially on hot, bright days are the cooling shadows of a dock.

While deep lake or impoundment fish still gravitate to docks, these man-made structures don't have nearly the attraction of docks on shallow lakes.

Weed beds are a key to finding bass. Common weeds found in virtually every lake and impoundment in America are hydrilla, millfoil, coontail and water cabbage. Almost all aquatic insects live in or close by these types of weeds. Minnows and other baitfish congregate in weedy areas to feed. Bass gravitate to weedy areas to take advantage of the congregated food supply. Weeds grow best in shallower water, where lighting is strongest. Bass hold in shallows for this reason.

Lily pads are probably the image conjured up by anyone imagining the surface of a bass lake. However, they are only good for hiding bass in lakes that have no other type of cover. Bass seem to prefer holding to alternate structure if it is available. Edges of lily pads are giveaways to anglers that a drop-off is near, as pads grow out to the edges of drop-offs. These pad edges/drop-offs are ideal bass holding areas.

Standing timber in a reservoir or downed trees are bass favorites, although they are the most difficult areas to fish because of snags. Locating bass in timber can be tricky, depending upon how thick the trees are. If timber is thick bass will not be in the middle of it, rather they tend to gravitate toward the edges. Conversely, if trees or logs are sparse, look for bass in the thickest portion of the timber. In reservoirs edges of standing timber can signal an old creek or road bed, ideal holding areas for bass. If you have a choice fish, fallen timber in areas dominated by standing timber. Bass feel safer laying under structure rather than alongside it. Also, downed timber creates more shade.

Putting it all together, finding bass by temperature, time of year, structure and location of foods, is what catches fish. There is no substitute for personal experience- predicting bass movements and recognizing holding areas on your favorite waters can only come with time spent on the water. You have to put in a lot of coins before you can expect to hit the jackpot.

Boat docks are favorite targets for bass fishermen. Docks provide shade, attract smaller baitfish, provide cover from predators and usually offer escape to deeper water.

Chapter 3

Basic Presentations For Stillwater Bass

Once you have learned how to find bass the next step is to practice basic methods for presenting lures. We call these methods "techniques". Bass fishing technique is defined as a specific combination of rods, reels, lines and lures in a certain type of water, used in a proven way to tempt fish to strike.

There are seemingly countless specialized methods of presenting lures, each presented with different gear, terminal riggings, depth and speed. As we will see in Chapter Four, each popular artificial bait has its own technique that makes it more effective, however, there are four basic presentations that the beginning bass angler should learn: flipping, pitching, dabbling and skipping. These four are fairly simple to learn, are possibly the most effective for solving special situations and apply to almost any lure.

Flipping and Pitching

Since the mid-1970s, when Dee Thomas coined "flipping", the name he gave to a technique he popularized in B.A.S.S. tournaments, his innovative technique has become undoubtedly the most popular and easiest employed by bass anglers. Flipping can be used anytime bass are laying in shallow water (5 feet or less) with limited visibility and/or in cover that requires an accurate presentation.

Flipping is done very close to where bass are laying, no more than 6 to 10 feet from your position. Not only is stealth a priority, but you can see the importance of having some cloudiness in the water to hide your approach. Basically, when flipping for bass at close range, your casts will be more accurate and, because you are so close, line stretch is at a minimum which translates to light bites being felt easily and hooksets of less force. The flipping method can be used with jigging spoons, Gitzits, plastic worms, marabou jigs, lead head jigs with plastic skirts, pork rinds and even spinnerbaits. Flipping also allows these lures to enter the water quietly.

The Technique

To "flip", position your boat or your body (flipping works well off docks and also from shore) within 10 feet of your target area. Position your rod tip at approximately 10 o'clock, then peel 3 or 4 feet of line off your reel with your free, or reeling hand. Leave a rod's length of line (approximately 7 to 9 feet) hanging from rod tip to lure and begin to swing the lure toward you, at the same time pull the line

Step 1.

Step 2.

toward you as if you were pulling back a drawstring on a bow. The lure should be swinging just above the water's surface. When the lure has reached the bottom of the swing, sharply drop your rod tip down towards the target to increase speed.

As the lure starts to swing forward, raise your rod again swiftly to the 10 o'clock position. Doing this shoots the lure forward. When the lure has started to swing upwards, lower the rod toward the target to allow the lure to enter the water quietly. After the lure has hit the surface, continue to lower the rod and feed line held in your free hand back through

the guides. This allows lures to sink straight down and not be pulled back toward you. Working lures vertically like this keeps them in the bass' range of vision longer, increasing chances for a strike. Remember, it is important that the lure be kept close to the water on the swing so it does not enter with a loud splash.

There will be times when you cannot get close enough to bass-holding structure to flip. Clear, shallow water and skittish bass are the culprits. However, tight cover still dictates that you make accurate casts. This situation calls for pitching. Pitching is basically the same technique as flipping, the only difference is that it is done from a farther distance, from 15 to 30 feet from your position.

Proper rod and casting position for pitching. Notice in photo above that the cast initiates with the bait in the angler's hand.

The Technique

Start with the rod tip pointed at the water, almost touching the surface. Let out a rod's length of line. Grasp the lure with your free hand, holding it near the butt section of your rod, making sure your line is tight but not so tight that it puts any bend in the rod tip. Keep your reel in the free-spool position if employing a level-wind, or bail in the open position for spinning reels. Now, simultaneously, lift the rod swiftly while letting go of the lure. This causes the lure to rapidly swing down and shoot forward towards the target water. By feathering the reel spool with your thumb (with a

level-wind) or stopping the line with a forefinger or free hand (with a spinning reel), you can easily control distance and accuracy. Again, after the cast is made, drop the rod tip to ensure the lure enters quietly.

In limited visibility conditions it may require a few more casts into an area when pitching. Due to greater distances from target water, lures are not able to be worked vertically. A swifter-moving lure has less chance to be seen, or felt by bass. Odds are that if a section requires 5 casts when flipping, it may take 10 to work thoroughly when pitching. The same types of lures mentioned earlier that work for flipping also work for pitching.

Unlike other bass techniques where a swift lunge to the bait is easily felt by the angler, the slow, methodical presentations of flipping and pitching more often than not elicit soft takes from bass. You must learn to watch your line for slight twitches or hesitations, or be ready for the faintest bumps transmitted to the hand. Here the old adage rings loud, "jerk or be one". If you think a bass has grabbed the lure, set the hook. Often it is nothing or a snag, but that "snag" can sometimes turn out to be a half dozen pounds of airborne bucketmouth.

Dabbling

Since bass display a tendency to lay under, alongside and behind thick cover when it is available, there will be situations when even super-accurate presentations like flipping and pitching won't get the lure in front of them. The only way to present a bait to these heavy cover bass is to literally drop it straight down to them. Trophy-sized bass and bass that have been subjected to heavy pressure also tend to gravitate to the thickest cover available.

Positioning your boat as close to the holding areas (obstructions) as possible is the key to successful dabbling.

Even though dabbling is a technique you will rarely use, it is important to practice as it allows you to get to these fish when no other method is viable.

The Technique

Dabbling is possibly the simplest bass technique and requires a stealthy approach and a bit of color to the water to cloak your approach, because you must get within 5 to 6 feet from your target water. Dabbling works best in water from 2 to 10 feet deep.

Position the rod tip straight out and directly above the opening of brush, pads, weeds, etc., and slowly lower the lure, slow enough so that the slightest disturbance is made entering the water. Drop the bait down slowly, in 12 inch increments—a deliberately falling offering is interpreted as being unaware of the bass' presence and therefore easy to approach. Watch your line as many bass take the lure on the fall. Because this is a slow, deliberate presentation like flipping and pitching, a majority of takes will be soft, a twitch in the line or a slight bump is all you feel. Set the hook immediately if you suspect something has grabbed the bait. After the lure has reached bottom bring up a foot of line and begin to rhythmically raise and lower the rod tip 4 to 6 inches to give life to the lure. Work the bait back toward the surface like this, then drop it back down and repeat.

Because you will be fishing vertically and slowly in heavy weeds, edges of lily pads, tree limbs and/or heavy brush, dabbling is best done with weedless jigs or worms. Unlike spinnerbaits or plugs, these baits require minimum movement to impart fish-attracting action.

Keep in mind that dabbling, like pitching and flipping, is most effective when there is some color to the water to hide your approach; also during spring spawning season (and autumn) when bass are in shallow water to lay eggs and feed. Of course, when water conditions are gin clear, dabbling is almost impossible because you cannot get close enough to lower baits without spooking fish.

Skipping

Back in the early 1970s, Kentucky professional bassman Ron Shearer came up with a most effective technique for hooking "unreachable" bass. He found that when bass lay under cover, such as overhanging branches, conventional lob casting could not go far enough under obstructions to entice reluctant bass to come out and strike. The solution was a cast that would skip a bait, much the same as a flat rock, across the surface at a low trajectory. This presented the bait closer to the fish. "Skipping" was born, and it is one of the most versatile presentations a basser can learn.

Overhanging limbs are not the only situation requiring skipping. Docks, both floating and on pilings, are prime skipping targets. Undercut banks and flooded treetops are also good areas to skip. Any time bass move into and under structure, skipping is a viable technique to reach them. When executed properly you can skip a lure up to 15 feet under an overhanging obstacle. As a bonus you can skip for bass in all degrees of visibility from clear to murky.

The Technique

Skipping is the most difficult cast to master. Considerable practice is the key, not for simply skipping the bait, but learning to be accurate *after* the lure starts to skip. A few inches of clearance between the overhanging object and the water line is plenty of room to skip a bait. Start with the rod pointed back and away from the target, slightly lower than waist high. When making the cast, snap the rod tip forward, at the same time bringing the tip down toward the surface. This hard forward snap down towards the water causes the bait to shoot out parallel to the water line. The distance, or how many skips across the water you achieve, is relative to how hard you throw the lure and how low a trajectory you make the cast. Remember, practice skipping until you get a feel for how hard to cast each type of lure so it lands approximately where you want it to.

How far you can skip a lure is directly related to the type of reel you choose. Since a skipped lure stops in its tracks after a few bounces, unless you are gifted with great touch on a casting (level-wind) reel, you will get backlashes. By using a spinning reel, you can throw a bait harder, skipping it farther than is possible with a level-wind. There is no chance for line fouling with spinning gear.

Lures for skipping range from traditional plastic worms and bullet-head slip sinkers to Gitzits, Slug-Gos and top water lures. The best surface condition for skipping is mirror smooth, yet you can still skip when there is a slight chop. 🐟

Skipping

Chapter 4

Most Popular Lures and Their Techniques

Now that we've discussed basic techniques—flipping and pitching, dabbling and skipping—we can concentrate on the most popular artificial lures and techniques that work best for each.

We've chosen to eliminate live baits from this book for several reasons. Although possibly no lure ever manufactured can tempt bass as well as the real thing, live baits can be difficult to obtain in many areas and are truly a pain to keep fresh and alive. Real bait is not allowed in professional bass fishing tournaments, and even though the majority of bass fishermen have no ambition of joining the professional ranks, keep in mind that most fishermen do release their bass. Live baits are more often than not taken deeply which makes the option of releasing that fish iffy. Deeply-hooked fish bleed easily. On the other hand, bass rarely swallow artificial lures and are hooked superficially in the outer edges of the mouth. It is more of a conservation issue than one of effectiveness. However, if an angler takes the time to work an artificial to its maximum degree of efficiency, he will hook nearly as many bass as the person choosing live baits.

The question has often been raised, "What does a lure represent to a bass?" Do they lash out at a lure because it mimics a familiar food, or do they strike out of territorial anger? Many studies have been done and experts agree that bass are simply opportunistic feeders, anything that has the right smell, vibration and color for the present conditions will trigger a reaction. We do know that bass are only territorial when guarding spawning areas, other than these times bass don't seem too bothered by intrusions of their space. Since most biologists and bass pros don't agree on what a lure represents (and bass do not talk), we can only choose what has been successful over the years.

This chapter deals with the four most popular artificial bass lures: plastic worms, spinnerbaits, crankbaits and jigs. These were picked by a combination of which baits are highly touted by leading bass professionals and by general effectiveness in the greatest range of conditions. While there are dozens of other "specialty baits" available to the bass fisherman, the beginner will do well with these choices anywhere bass are found.

Plastic Worms

Ask any tournament bass angler which artificial lure he would choose if made to fish just one, and the answer would likely be unanimous: plastic worms. Since Nick Creme originated the first soft-plastic worms back in 1949, no other bait has won more tournaments, caught more bass and is more versatile. It's a fact that plastic worms have caught as many bass as all other types of artificial lures combined.

Obviously, a plastic worm represents just that, a nightcrawler. There is scarcely a freshwater game fish in America that turns up its nose at a worm. What makes worms such a

Plastic worms come in 4 to 12 inch sizes and in hundreds of colors and color combinations.

"killer" for bass is that it is a silent bait. Because a worm moves as a living creature—undulating, crawling, writhing, etc.—it doesn't make the disturbance of a spinnerbait or crankbait, something a bass may associate with danger. The beauty of worm fishing is because real worms move so little, anglers do not need to impart a lot of action to illicit strikes. This makes the plastic worm a fine choice for beginning bass anglers.

The plastic worm is probably the most effective lure for large, wary bass. Whereas small bass attack any lure that looks edible, large bass do not get to be that size by being careless. Because a worm so closely resembles a real, living creature, the old and wise fish will readily approach with full interest.

Choosing Worm Sizes, Colors and Riggings

Which sizes and colors of plastic worms are most effective? Well, if just one size and color were enough to tempt bass year-round in all ranges of temperatures, visibility and structure, tackle companies would have to eliminate 99% of their lines. Fortunately for them, there are times when changing worm sizes and colors make the difference.

Worms sizes range from tiny 4 inchers to 12-inch snake replicas. They normally are made with two types of tails: flat, paddle-shaped like a natural nightcrawler, or curly-tailed to give the illusion of "swimming" when worked through the water. For cold water situations (58 degrees or less), a flat-tailed worm with little action is the choice. When bass are

slowed down by low metabolism, a slow-moving, slight action worm gets the bites. When water temperatures are higher (above 75 degrees), bass are active and a worm with maximum action—the curly-tail—can draw bass from a greater range and can be fished faster to cover more water.

Size is possibly the most important factor in choosing worms. Standard thinking is to match worms to the size of your quarry. If you expect to be hooking bass in the 1 to 4 pound category, then a smaller worm (4 to 5 inches) will get more pickups. If, say, you are fishing in a Florida or California lake with expectations of bass weighing in double digits, then a larger worm (6 to 9 inches) is the choice.

First, if possible, match worm sizes to foods bass are keying on. As far as beginners are concerned, 90% of the time a 5 to 7 inch worm catches bass in virtually any condition. However, you will run into situations and conditions that call for a longer or shorter worm.

For clear water, spooky fish and light tackle, drop to a 4 incher. When fishing in heavy moss an 8-incher may be a better choice as it casts a larger profile (to be more easily seen) and won't be completely hidden when fishing over bottom-growing weeds. Secondly, look at the type of structure you will be fishing. Larger worms over 7 inches tend to wrap their tails on branches and brush and break. Smaller worms (4 to 6 inches) in these heavy brush situations tend to work freely rather than hang up. When water is cloudy, a larger worm makes a greater disturbance which aids bass in finding the lure. Also, a curly-tailed worm adds to vibration in stained water. The trick is to keep several sizes and tail styles handy for matching conditions.

Which colors are most effective? Doug Hannon, leading expert on bass behavior, claims a bass has the greatest range of vision for the color red. Using red worms then, you may think, would result in more pickups. Hardly the case when examining tackle boxes of touring bass pros. If you keep track of colors preferred by professionals, the order goes like this, from favorite on down: purple, black, motor oil (a sort of greenish/dark brown), brown, red and green. The most popular and effective color is purple by a large margin; why this color works so well is not known. Black and motor oil are a close second in garnering strikes. If you stick with those three colors—purple, black and motor oil—you can catch bass in all temperatures. For conditions under limited visibility to murky, two colored worms (often labeled "fire tails") seem to produce more strikes. Red tails are the most common with chartreuse a close second.

The author's favorite "searching" worm: a 4 inch, black with a chartreuse tail.

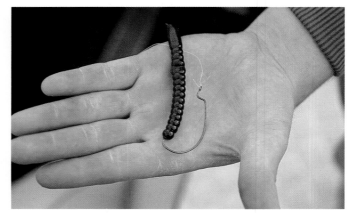

*Three steps for Texas rigging worms. **STEP 1:** The hook is inserted 1/4 to 1/2 inch through the center of the head . . .*

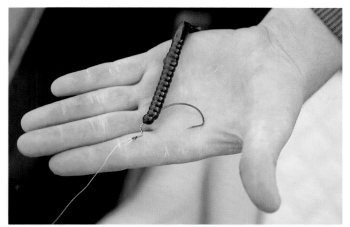

STEP 2: . . . the hook is drawn through the head and turned so it lines up with the "seam" on the worm and . . .

STEP 3: . . . the hook tine is inserted back into the body of the worm until the hook point barely escapes the skin.

Rigging the Worm

There are two basic ways to rig plastic worms: the Texas rig and the weedless rig. For the majority of bass anglers the Texas rigging is standard and most popular.

The Texas rig is a weedless, non-snaggy hookup. Start by inserting the hook point in the center of the tip of the worm's head. Push the hook approximately 1/2 to 3/4 of an inch into the worm head, then push the tine and barb out the side of the head. Push the worm head up the shank of

the hook until it barely covers the eye. Turn the hook until the point faces the center of the body and insert the point until it is tissue paper-thickness from poking through the other side. Make sure that the worm hangs straight after it has been rigged. Any bumps or twists in the worm make it unnatural looking and make it easier for the worm to hang up. After the worm is pegged on the hook straight, you are ready to fish the Texas rig. Once you have practiced hooking a plastic worm this way, it will only take a few moments to do it each time.

The second way to hook a worm is on a weedless hook. Attaching the worm onto a weedless wire-guard style hook is easier than Texas rigging and does allow for easier hooksets, because the hook point doesn't have to be pushed through plastic.

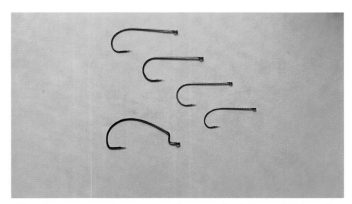

The four common sizes of correct styles of thin-wire worm hooks, top to bottom: #3/0 (top). #2/0, #1/0 and #1 (bottom). The hook on the bottom left is a wide gap style worm hook for use with Slug-Gos.

Hook sizes must match the size of the worm. As you might expect, small worms work best with small hooks and large worms work best with larger hooks. Short, thin-profile worms from 4 to 5 inches match with #1 and #1/0s; 6 inch worms pair with #1/0 and #2/0s while 7 to 9 inch worms work best with a #3/0. Keep in mind that smaller hooks are easier to set and do less damage.

Since plastic worms are not heavy enough to cast nor sink on their own, you must add some weight. The bullet-type slip sinker is the route to go. The slip sinker does three things for the worm fisherman: one, provides weight for casting and getting the worm down to the bass; two, keeps the worm straight on the hook and protects the head from rocks and other abrasives and three, allows anglers to feel exactly where and how the worm is working.

Which weight is best to use? There is no one weight for all worm fishing. There are variables to consider. First, consider temperature. Lighter weighted worms fall slower and are more likely to be taken by a lethargic bass, while a heavier weighted worm sinks faster. In warmer water conditions high metabolism bass are more likely to hit a faster moving worm. The greater the depth, the more weight needed—not only to get worms down to bass but the more line out, the less feel you have. Increased weight makes up for line stretch and distance. Line diameter is also a factor; thicker lines sink slower due to increased water resistance. The thinner the diameter of line used, the faster worms sink with less weight.

If you wish to work worms in relatively shallow water or over snaggy bottoms a light weight is all that is required.

Lighter weights make it more difficult for a bass to jump and throw the hook, also the less weight a bass feels when it picks up a worm the less it feels something is wrong. Also, you have to factor in wind; sometimes you have to add weight as the wind blows harder. A rule of thumb used by professionals is to use the lightest sinker that works for the conditions.

For matching weights with worm size, here are some common pairings: 4, 5 and 6 inch worms, 3/16 or 1/8th ounce for shallow water (2 to 8 feet) or drifting over obstructions, in water of medium depth (8 to 15 feet) use 1/4 to 3/8th ounce and in rare deep water conditions (over 20 feet), try 3/4 ounce. Seven, 8 and 9 inch worms need slightly heavier weights, from 1/8th in shallow water to 1/4 and 3/8th ounces for deeper situations.

hook home. It's not so easy when worming. Bass take worms with a subtle sucking in, or flaring of the gills. As soon as you realize that a bass has inhaled your worm, you need to set the hook with some power. Hooksets are not too complicated. All the bass angler has to do on the first signal of a take is immediately lower the rod tip toward the fish, rapidly reel in all slack and quickly sweep the rod straight up.

Hard hooksets are standard with heavier lines (12 pound test and up), and they accomplish several things. One, it takes a lot of transferred force to push the point through the worm (when Texas rigged) and into the bony plates of a bass' mouth. Two, a swift, hard set tends to pull bass away from their lairs and keeps them from tangling your line in obstructions.

An example of a properly Texas rigged worm and weight.

Split shotting with tiny 4 inch worms is by far the most productive method for finding bass under difficult conditions.

b) Basic Worm Technique

Besides being one of the most effective artificial baits, worms are undoubtedly the easiest to fish. Even though there are a dozen variations to the worming technique, there is one basic way to work worms. For the beginner this may be the best method to start with.

Begin by determining your target (bass holding area) and cast the worm into that area. Allow the worm to settle to the bottom, while it is sinking try to keep most of the slack out of the line, yet not so much that you accidentally pull the worm out of position. You want to keep out most of the slack so you can feel a bass taking the worm on the drop, which is actually quite common. Be alert for slight movements in the line, such as twitching or movement to one side, perhaps you may even feel faint bumps. All these movements mean a bass has nabbed the worm on the fall.

When the worm has hit bottom or achieved desired depth, hold the rod at a 9 o'clock position with the tip pointed at the worm. Slowly reel in all slack. When the line becomes tight and the worm is just about to be lifted out of position, begin to raise the rod tip with a slow, deliberate lift until the tip points to 12 o'clock and allow the worm to again settle. Repeat until the worm is worked back to your position.

Most lures with a great deal of action, like crankbaits and spinnerbaits, are taken with gusto by bass and setting the hook is done for you or merely tightening the line sinks the

Split shotting

Bass anglers out West can claim fame to this worm technique. Even though westerners have accepted this technique, there are many who still strongly believe this light-tackle method is not nearly as effective as claimed. Not only is split shotting one of—if not the most—effective worming techniques, it catches bass when all other techniques fail.

Split shotting tackle consists of basically this: terminal outfits are 4 inch curly-tailed plastic worms with small split-shot placed 18 to 24 inches above. Used in tandem with 6-pound line, split shotting is definitely a light-line, finesse method. It is a technique practiced in shallow water (15 feet or less) with a constantly moving bait. Being a cast and retrieve technique, an angler can work areas quicker which helps in locating concentrations of moving fish. The beauty of split shotting is that by employing light line and a 4 inch worm, you get the attention of both aggressive and reluctant bass—the smaller worm always produces takes when seemingly nothing else in the tackle box works.

Split shotting works well in several situations. When unstable weather patterns or lake levels change, making bass move and become unaggressive, you can still find fish. When you are on lakes with heavy boat traffic, either by recreational boaters that scare fish or many anglers putting day-long pressure over bass, the 4 inch worm and light line still gets bites. Wary bass holding in clear, shallow water are prime candidates for split shotting.

Using ultra-light equipment when split shotting shows off the fight of any bass, especially scrappy smallmouth like this 2 1/2 pounder.

. . . until slack is reeled up and the process is repeated.

To split shot position your boat at a workable casting distance from your target water, say 15 to 30 feet away. When fishing in shallow water conditions, you will be casting toward shore into shallower water, working the worm out into deeper water. After making the cast, and your worm has settled onto bottom, point the rod tip down towards the water and in the direction of the worm, at roughly a 5 o'clock position. Reel in slack and slowly draw the worm along, pulling the rod tip back 2 to 3 feet in the opposite direction of your worm. Return the rod to the 5 o'clock position, at the same time reeling in the few feet of slack. Reel, draw, reel—repeat until the worm is worked back to your position.

When you are split shotting properly, you will feel the shot bumping off bottom every few feet. Doing this keeps the worm working a few inches off bottom, which not only keeps the bait within the bass' cone of vision, the curly tail simulates a crawling creature or baitfish. Standard shot sizes are a #4 for calm water and a larger #2 shot when there is wind. Removable split shot are a no-no, as the "wings" make the shot snag prone.

Rigging the worm is important when split shotting. Use the standard Texas rigging with a thin-wire #1 Aberdeen hook. Pay close attention to the "line" running down the length of the worm. Push the hook into the center of the seam. This ensures the worm is working straight up and down and the tail is not swimming sideways.

Strikes when split shotting are subtle. When a bass inhales the tiny plastic worm, you feel nothing more than a hesitation, minute "thump" or most often merely a spongy feeling of resistance.

The thin, sharp Aberdeen hook and light line dictate a different type of hookset when split shotting. When resistance is felt from a bass, by keeping the line tight, the rod tip down and sweeping it in a steady, swift motion it is easy to drive the hook home.

Even though split shotting has a reputation for hooking only smaller fish, this statement isn't entirely true. Split shotting takes bass up to 6 pounds consistently. Besides, it's better to be hooking some fish in difficult conditions than none at all.

Proper rod positioning for split shotting. Note that during the presentation, the rod tip is drawn along only 2 to 3 feet . . .

Slack-Lining

Since inactive and non-receptive bass seem to be the order rather than the exception, there are methods of presenting a plastic worm to these reclusive bass that get takes. Slack-lining gets strikes when bass are not feeding, non-active or subject to heavy pressure.

Also called "dead-sticking", "dead-worming", "doin' nuthin", etc., it is the best worming technique when bass are shut off. For some reason no expert has been able to explain why bass sometimes prefer a worm that doesn't move. The best explanation to date has to do with water temperatures. During early spring cold-water periods (less than 60 degrees), bass are lethargic and will not move far or aggressively for a lure. On the opposite end, when water temperatures rise above 80 degrees, depleted oxygen makes bass loggy and non-responsive. In addition, if you are sure that there are bass in the target area, you have a better chance at finding them by fishing slowly and thoroughly. This technique is exactly as it sounds—the worm moves as little as possible and sometimes not at all.

To "slack-line", move within approximately 20 feet (the closer the better) of your target area. Cast the worm alongside the target and allow it to sink on a totally slack line. Any tightness of the line caused by either wind or your not feeding enough line to the falling worm causes it to sink at an angle away from the target. Leave the worm near the holding area for 15 to 30 seconds. Slowly lift the rod tip and move the worm a few inches to a few feet and repeat the waiting process. Try not to lift the worm out of position, simply tighten up the line enough to move it ever so slowly to another position, and again give some slack. Keep enough slack so that it hangs between your rod tip and the water in a crescent bow and keep a sharp eye on it. If the line twitches or tightens, it's a bass. The trick to this technique is patience.

Sometimes there is more current in a body of water than you think. Wind and even boat traffic can cause enough water movement to make a worm wobble ever so slightly. This mini-current imparts more than enough action to attract lethargic bass.

Best worm styles and sizes to use vary depending on clarity. For clear water use a smaller 4 inch worm; in limited or cloudy conditions use a larger worm from 6 to 8 inches. Most bass experts that employ this technique agree that a plain-tailed worm has plenty of action. Curly-tailed worms can give too much movement but may be just the ticket in limited visibility when just a bit more motion can trigger strikes. Experiment on your home waters to determine which works best for you.

Since you want the worm to fall and lay on the bottom as naturally and slowly as possible, only the smallest amount of lead is required. One-sixteenth of an ounce is generally plenty. How you place the weight on or near the worm depends on the type of structure you are fishing. If there is mud or rock on bottom rig the lead (the standard bullet slip sinker) normally, or resting on the worm head. If there is, for example, a foot of vegetation on bottom, place the lead 14 to 16 inches above the worm. Rigging lead so that worms may float above weeds allows bass to find them easily and permits worms to work freely in the current.

Strikes when slack-lining are slight, almost imperceptible takes. Often your line will twitch or move slightly to one side. Takes are common on the drop as the worm sinks nat-

Slack-lining tricked this deep-water pre-spawn largemouth.

urally. This is the main reason for keeping some slack at all times after the cast is made. If the bass has been stung recently by a hook or is not particularly hungry and just "pecking", you may feel no more than a hesitation in the drop. Strike any time you suspect a bass may have the worm.

Two most popular styles of worm rattles: (Left) "brass and glass", brass worm weights with glass beads and (right) small plastic hollow inserts filled with tiny metal rattles.

A soft monofilament, unlike stiffer line, allows the worm to fall naturally and lay on the bottom in a natural position. Stiff lines may develop memory coils that pull worms out of position or fall at an unnatural angle.

Remember to give slack-lining or dead-sticking a try in early season and during the hotter dog-days of summer.

Rattling Worms

You will find situations when worming that joining sound to an already seductive visual helps trigger strikes. A "rattle" added to the worm can produce bass when plain worms get nary a touch.

What is a worm rattle? There are several variations, some you put together yourself and one that is commercially available. Your first options are home-made rattles, three types in particular. First, try placing a round 5mm to 9mm glass or plastic bead (most professionals prefer glass because it makes a louder "tick") between the sliding bullet weight and the worm head/hook eye. The second option is to employ two sliding weights, obviously two lighter sliding leads than one normally chosen for the conditions. The two leads "clack" together as the worm is worked through the water. Your third and possibly best combination for home-made rattles are "glass and brass", or simply one glass bead next to a brass bead. The word from the pros is that glass and brass beads together produce the loudest "click".

The style of rattles you may purchase are small 1/2 to 3/4 inch thin plastic tubes containing 3 to 4 tiny glass, plastic or metal BB's. These are called "arrow rattles" as they have a pointed end making them easy to insert into a soft plastic worm body. Ideal placement for these rattles is in the head of the worm, just above the area where the hook point should protrude.

There are four specific times when rattles are important additions to worms. First, and most important, is when visibility is limited in stained or murky water. Rattles can literally call to bass, enabling them to find worms when vision is handicapped. Second, whenever probing heavy cover. Bass

hear the "clicking" beads up to 5 feet away, alerting it that something is in its vicinity, even though it cannot yet see the object through branches, millfoil, grass, etc. Bass will search out the source of the vibration. Your third consideration is in cold water containing lethargic fish. Sound can often be just the incentive non-aggressive bass need to pick up a worm. Finally, when fishing over pre-spawn or spawning bass, a rattling worm seems to provoke a strike better than plain worms.

You may find rattling worms so effective under all worming conditions that you'll rarely fish them any other way.

Slug-Gos

A relatively new bait, the Slug-Go is appropriately named as it closely mimics in shape those slimy garden pests, sans antennae. Most popular sizes are the 4-1/2 and 6 inch varieties. The Slug-Go is an elongated "jerk" bait with a rounded top and flat bottom. This odd configuration is what imparts action to these long, fat "worms", its flat bottom and 90 degree edges give it an eye-catching side-to-side slow wobble. What they represent to bass is strictly a guess, a wounded baitfish seems to be the common theory.

Slug-Gos are also unusual in that they are fished with no additional weight. Weight kills the action that makes the Slug-Go so deadly. Created from a thick slab of plastic, they have enough weight to be cast effectively.

Slug-Gos are rigged much the same as plastic worms, the Texas rigging being most effective. However, because the bait is wide, a larger, wide gap style hook must be used because it has to penetrate a thicker lure body than a standard plastic worm. Slug-Gos must be rigged straight, with zero bend in the body to ensure its trademark erratic movement. When rigging the lure hook it Texas style, except leave the hook point barely exposed instead of just inside the body. Because of the thickness of the lure this exposed point allows for an easier and more efficient hookset. For the 4-1/2 inch bait, a #3/0 fine wire wide gap worm hook matches well, and for the 6 inch Slug-Go pair it with a #4/0 to #5/0.

There are two ways to fish Slug-Gos. First, they can be used as a surface lure, much the same as a lipless crankbait. When fishing them on the surface keep in mind that they do sink, so your rod angle must be greater, at approximately 11 o'clock, and your speed of retrieve has to be faster to keep it on or just beneath the surface film.

Secondly, undoubtedly the most popular way to fish the Slug-Go, is to let it sink naturally, or give the bait a quick twitch with the rod tip every five to ten seconds to add a bit of action. When the Slug-Go slowly falls, it "slides" a few feet to one side before flipping over and gliding in the opposite direction. This sideways glide makes it ideal for skipping under or alongside docks, as the lure sinks it travels further under to hard-to-reach fish. Experiment with different rod positions and frequency of movements. Often the best method for fishing the Slug-Go is to combine all methods, that is to fish it slow, fast, on top and on a free-fall all in one retrieve. Whichever point of the varied retrieve a bass strikes, you then know which technique to concentrate on. The majority of takes occur while the lure is on the free-fall.

You can control, to a degree, how fast your Slug-Go sinks by varying line pound test. The heavier and thicker monofilament you use, the more water resistance and slower sink

Two most popular sizes of Slug-Gos: the 4-1/2 inch (top) and the 3 inch (bottom).

you will experience. Heavier lines also inhibit action, so if you desire more action or a more rapid sink from your lure stay with lighter pound tests.

Because Slug-Gos sink slowly and are normally presented at crawl speed, they are ideal for shallow water duty. Besides docks, they can be fished in, around and under any structure, over rock points, sunken trees and brush or even hopped over pads. The best condition for employing Slug-Gos seems to be for pre-spawn/spawning shallow water bass.

Concerning color, dark bodies get the vote. Smoke/gold flake, smoke/silver flake, olive and motor oil are excellent choices. Slug-Gos, because of their large profile, definitely qualify as a big fish bait.

Some examples of spinnerbaits. The bass angler can choose different weight, arm lengths, blade finishes, sizes, number of blades and skirt colors to match all conditions.

Spinnerbaits

A spinnerbait is basically a lead jig head with a hook attached to a V-shaped length of heavy-gauge wire adorned with one or two metal spinner blades and a rubber skirt. Spinnerbaits are a must for a bass angler's lure collection. What these bizarre contraptions are supposed to simulate in the food chain is anyone's guess; (perhaps a crayfish or forage fish) what is certain is bass find them most appealing. Next to the plastic worm spinnerbaits are the most popular and productive artificial bass lure.

Spinnerbaits are most effective in warm-water conditions. Although you can catch bass on them in all tempera-tures, the best temperature range is from 56 to 75 degrees—when fish are most active and aggressive. Spinnerbaits are also a good shallow water lure, best used in depths from 3 to 12 feet where actively feeding, aggressive or staging spawning bass call home.

For shallow water spinnerbait work lead heads should weigh 1/8, 1/4 and 1/2 ounce. Most professionals prefer the 1/4 ounce lure as it is the most versatile. By simply adjusting line angle and speed of retrieve, 1/4 ounce spinnerbaits can be worked at any—or all—levels in that 3 to 12 foot range.

You have the choice of fishing either long-armed or short-armed spinnerbaits. Long-arm 'baits have the top portion of the arm extending past the hook point, while short-armed baits simply don't reach as far. Long-armed spinnerbaits are best when fishing heavy cover as they tend to protect the hook point better and keep weeds from fouling blades. Short-armed spinnerbaits are most effective in open water (small chance for a snag) where bass have a clearer shot at hook points.

To make spinnerbaits work at their maximum efficiency, be aware of a few tips. One, be sure your spinnerbait is "in tune". Look down on the top of the spinnerbait. The blade must be lined up with the tine (point) of the hook. Wire bodies can be accidentally bent from use, causing the lure to lean off-balance or cause the revolving blade to hit the hook point, possibly dulling it and/or impeding proper blade spin. Make sure your spinnerbaits come equipped with quality ball-bearing swivels on the blade. They may be a bit more expensive, however a free-spinning blade has more flash, vibration and can be worked with ease at slower speeds. The swivel eliminates possible line damaging twist and most importantly allows the blade to begin spinning immediately upon entering the water.

Hooks are positioned directly above the blade(s), point facing up. This allows the spinnerbait to come in contact with obstructions and not hang up, in addition this positioning puts the hook point near the flashing/vibrating blade—the spot targeted by a striking bass.

Choosing Blades, Finishes, Colors and Riggings

Blades

Typical styles and sizes for spinnerbaits are #4 or #5 French or Colorado (egg-shaped and almost round) blades. These wide profile blades create maximum "push" when retrieved, causing the blade to rise and ride high, a desirable characteristic when working shallow water or near the surface. Larger blades, such as a #5 or #6 not only create more lift but also transfer greater vibration to the rod tip, telegraphing to the angler exactly how fast the blade is spinning when the spinnerbait is not visible. Also, due to the lift provided by larger blades you can make a slower presentation.

If you want to work a spinnerbait deeper or faster, then smaller blades such as #2's (smallest) or #3's are good choices; they do not create as much lift or resistance. When employing spinnerbaits in limited visibility or murky water stick with a smaller blade. In these conditions bass rely on vibrations to find food, not sight. Smaller blades spin faster sending out a higher frequency of waves than larger blades.

Even though the nearly round Colorado style is the blade of choice in 90% of spinner baitfishing, switching to a thinner profile blade such as an Indiana or willow leaf style may be necessary when confronted with thick weeds or grass. Thin blades tend to foul less than thicker ones. Keep in mind that vibrations are more difficult to feel when using thin profile blades.

Some spinnerbaits are manufactured with tandem blades, such as a #3 French style followed with a #5 or #6 willow leaf style placed directly behind the lead smaller blade. While this double-blade system does produce greater flash and is to a degree more weedless, professionals lean toward single blades because they produce more vibrations and don't seem to draw any less strikes than the double.

Blade Finishes

How you match your natural metal finishes to the proper sized blades for spinner baitfishing could mean the difference between lots of strikes and not a touch. To see why we have to look at different stages of water clarity, temperature and available lighting.

First, keep in mind that all game fish, bass included, have an attraction threshold, thus you want your blade to give off enough flash to excite or enrage fish into striking, yet not so much flash that you "over-stimulate" and frighten them instead. This is why it is very important to choose proper blade finishes.

The flash and profile of spinnerbaits make them wise choices when bass are lethargic during cold winter months.

Let's start with cold (53 to 58) water temperatures. As long as the water has 6 feet to unlimited visibility, choose a silver-plated blade. Only silver-plate—not nickel—has enough flash to entice or enrage a lethargic bass to move to take a spinnerbait. Unlike nickel, which absorbs 90% of available light, silver reflects 90% of the light, creating maximum flash.

When water has 1 to 2 feet of visibility stay with a silver-plated blade regardless of temperature. You still need the flash of silver to enlarge your attraction radius. Other good times for silver-plated blades are early morning and evening when available light is at a minimum and maximum flash is needed to attract bass.

When temperatures start to warm (58 to 66 degrees) you no longer need the flash of silver plate to draw strikes. As long as there is adequate visibility (from 2 to 6 feet) polished copper, electric brass or 24k gold-plating will do for the majority of your bass fishing. The flash of 24k gold, copper and electric brass is not as bright as silver plate, yet they still give off plenty of light during daylight hours.

When water temperatures are optimum (70 to 83 degrees) and bass are at peak activity, you now have to be aware of conditions so you do not step over the attraction threshold. In these temperatures, under clear water conditions (6 feet to unlimited visibility) choose a nickel-plated blade. Since nickel absorbs light, it actually appears partially black and gives off very little flash. Use nickel blades any time you are faced with bright light and clear, warm water.

When bass are at their peak of aggressiveness during this maximum activity range you may not need the intense flash of silver-plate during dawn or evening hours. Copper, gold or brass work fine. If you are fishing overcast or dark days in warm water conditions, 24k gold and copper work fine.

When water clarity ranges from just a few inches to a foot of visibility, blade finish no longer matters, as bass rely on vibrations to find their food rather than sight. If any finish has an advantage, it is matte black. Black gives off the most distinct silhouette in murky water. You may even want to experiment with glow-in-the-dark blades.

There is debate over hammered-finished blades providing more reflection than smooth finished ones. Nowhere have I found evidence of this. However, if you have confidence in one style finish over the other by all means stick with it.

Even though spinnerbaits come in every shade of the rainbow, basic colors, black and white, work as well as any choice.

Spinnerbait colors on painted lead heads and rubber skirts are probably the least important features of these lures. Judging by professional preferences there seem to be just a few basic colors that work in all conditions.

The best way to choose spinnerbait colors is again to break it down by degrees of visibility; some colors definitely show up better (or less) than others. When fishing murky or off-colored water (a few inches to a foot) use chartreuse. Chartreuse is the brightest color and one of the last to leave the color spectrum. Black is also a good choice, probably the best color under all temperatures, degrees of clarity and lighting.

Other popular colors when visibility ranges from 1-1/2 foot all the way to clear are yellow, white, red and blue in that order. Again, if one color produces well for you, stay with it. Confidence and presentation catches as many bass as matching colors to conditions.

Riggings for Spinnerbaits, Hooks, Skirts and Trailers

When tossing spinnerbaits you will find that some days bass are interested enough to follow the lure and nip at it but not aggressive enough to get the point of the hook, or are only lightly lip-hooked. When this occurs it can be an advantage to add a trailer hook. Trailer hooks are larger-eyed hooks that fit over the barb of the original hook and seat on the bottom of the bend. They stay in place with a small piece of rubber tubing or rubber "keeper". The trailer hook should be the same size as the original hook.

Ron Soden tempted this Potholes Reservoir largemouth into coming to the surface for a "gurgled" spinnerbait.

When fishing water containing obstructions or brush, position the trailer hook in an upwards position (like the original) to keep it snagless and weedless. If you are fishing open waters with little chance for snags, position the trailer hook pointing down. This "up-down" configuration is an almost sure-thing for a landed bass.

The three considerations for spinnerbait skirts are length, the direction they face and materials they are made from. When bass are aggressive and striking spinnerbaits with authority, a regular length skirt does fine. Short-striking or nipping fish can be tricked by trimming skirt length to even with or slightly above the hook bend. Positioning, rather than the direction skirts are placed onto spinnerbaits, is important. By putting the skirt on backwards, the "legs" will face in the opposite direction of the working lure. This increases action in the skirt, causing them to "pulse" as the lure is pulled through water.

Your choice for skirt materials are rubber and plastic. Rubber skirts are definitely chosen more often. They are more supple and impart more action. However, plastic skirts are more durable. Again, which to choose is your call. Skirt colors include black, green, white, chartreuse, blue or any combination of the five. A rule of thumb for color choice is brighter colors for off-colored or murky water and subtle colors for clear.

Trailers are added strips of either rubber, plastic or pork rind cut to the shape of a long snake tongue—supposed to resemble frog legs to a degree—and placed on the bend of the hook. Trailers serve several purposes: to add buoyancy to enable anglers to work spinnerbaits higher; to add an extra bit of profile and create movement for additional vibes in cloudy water. Trailers come in many colors; most popular being black, white, frog pattern and chartreuse.

Splashing/Gurgling and Sub-Surface Waking

All bass lures have specific presentations that make them more effective. Spinnerbaits are no exception; there are several techniques that take full advantage of blade flash, vibration and profile.

Spinnerbaits can be fished at many depths, but their best use is for shallow water duty. During spring or early summer (depending upon where you live), when water temperatures begin climbing above 58 degrees bass, particularly largemouth, begin to move into shallow water (3 to 12 feet) to feed and stage for spawning. At this time bass are aggressive and will slash at virtually any lure, especially one that creates quite a commotion. This is prime time for "gurgling", "splashing" or "waking" a spinnerbait on or just beneath the surface.

The Techniques

When bass are aggressive and laying near shallow cover such as sunken brush piles, stumps or weed beds, the gurgling technique allows you to draw these ravaging fish up and out of their tackle-eating lairs. This noise also draws them from greater distances, letting you work areas quicker—but thoroughly—with less casts, therefore giving yourself more chances for a hookup. Gurgling works best when there is a mirror water surface.

You gurgle and splash a spinnerbait by starting your retrieve the instant the lure hits water (perhaps even slightly before) and begin rapidly reeling. Reel fast enough so that the blade is half in and half out of the water. Hold the rod so the tip points between 11 and 12 o'clock. This angle keeps line out of the water and ensures spinnerbaits are always on or near the surface.

Quarter-ounce spinnerbaits perform best, as lighter weights are obviously easier to keep near the surface. Some professionals have switched to flat-headed weights on spinnerbaits—the smooth, flat surface creates a planing action that helps keep lures near the surface.

If a steady, swift surface retrieve does not produce a strike there are variances in spinnerbait techniques that may work better. "Hopping" spinnerbaits out of the water every few feet causes even more splashing and attraction. Oppositely, you can halt the spinnerbait in its tracks, stopping it dead in the water and allowing it to fall (every few feet or so) before again quickly reeling and resuming splashing. This dropping method works best after a bass has taken a shot at a gurgling spinnerbait and missed. Immediately dropping the lure gives the illusion (to the fish) that dinner is merely stunned. Bass will turn and whack the lure on the fall.

Sub-surface waking, or "bulging" the surface—that is keeping the blade just under the surface film, creating a bulge of water—works well when summer water temperatures range between 75 to 83 degrees. Instead of water flying from a gurgling lure, the sub-surface blade leaves a V shaped wake trailing behind. This wake resembles a wounded or fleeing baitfish. Rod angle is identical as when gurgling, however you must reel a bit slower to ensure spinner blades do not break the surface.

While sub-surface waking works best on a table-flat surface, don't abandon this technique when there is chop. Either switch to a spinnerbait with a larger blade, such as a #6 or even #7, or go with a tandem spin. These larger blades and/or double blades create a higher and wider bulge, making lures highly visible in sloppy conditions. Alternately dropping spinnerbaits is also effective when waking.

You can employ fairly heavy lines for spinner baitfishing for strikes can be savage and sudden. Heavier pound test lines create more water resistance making it easier to work spinnerbaits near the surface. When gurgling or waking, 99% of your line is out of the water and is not visible to bass. Spool up no less than 12 pound test; better yet choose 15 to 20 pound.

Fluttering and Dropping

Although spinnerbaits are probably at peak effectiveness when worked shallow, you should not abandon them when bass hold in deeper water. The slower presentations afforded by spinnerbaits have advantages over other lures in like situations. When bass are in colder water (53 to 58 degrees) or holding around deeper water structure, such as submerged trees or rocky ledges, fluttering and dropping spinnerbaits are choice weaponry for these semi-lethargic, deep-holding fish.

Your choices for these methods are short-arm 'baits with large blades, such as #6 or #7. Larger blades create greater resistance, therefore slowing down the lure. This slower

movement prevents the spinnerbait from dropping too swiftly. Shorter-armed spinnerbaits are better balanced for vertical presentations like this.

The Technique

Position yourself 15 to 40 feet from your target area. Cast beyond the structure—if possible—and allow the spinnerbait to fall on a moderately tight line until the lure hits that particular piece of cover. Now, raise the rod tip with a quick upwards motion until the spinnerbait clears the obstruction, then let it flutter and drop back down. The trick is to keep the line tight while allowing the lure to fall straight down. Repeat until bottom is reached or the lure works down past the fish holding depth. You can work steep banks and drop-offs up to 50 feet deep with this technique.

Always position the rod tip at 10 o'clock as strikes come at any time. With the rod in this position you are always ready to sweep upward and set a hook. You will find that most takes occur during the down-flutter.

Some examples of crankbaits. Crankbaits are the most animated and exciting of all artificial bass baits.

Crankbaits

Called "crankbaits" because they are just that- cranked back in after being cast—these are tried and true bass catchers. Crankbaits, more commonly known as diving plugs, are effective all year in a great variety of holding water situations. They attract bass from the surface down to 20 feet deep and more.

Made from highly-durable hollow plastic or painted/plastic coated wood, with the exception of lipless top water styles, all are designed to dive to varying depths and are supposed to resemble, to a degree, colors, shapes and sizes of forage fish. Even though crankbaits can be matched to predominant baitfish for a particular body of water, vibrations given off by plugs (their trademark side-to-side wobble) are what truly attracts bass to strike. It's these vibrations that make crankbaits the number one choice for covering the greatest amount of water in the shortest time.

Some crankbaits are designed to sink, some to suspend (neither float nor sink, just hold at whatever depth the plug was worked down to) and the majority to float. Some come equipped with rattles for even more fish-attracting sound. The floating and diving characteristics of crankbaits allow beginners to cover all depths, from the surface to the maximum depth the plug is designed to dive. Due to their big-lipped designs, crankbaits are naturally snag-resistant lures, as it's the lip that first comes in contact with obstructions and deflects the plug. For this reason floating plugs are most popular; if a crankbait momentarily hangs up, by simply releasing line tension it will float back to the surface.

How your crankbait runs during the retrieve is critical to success. Some brands of diving plugs wobble straight and true directly out of their bubble packaging, however, sometimes you get one that runs to one side. This creates an unnatural sideways swim or causes the plug to repeatedly flip over. You can correct this by "tuning" your plugs. For example, if the plug swings to the right, use a pair of needle-nosed pliers and twist the eye-screw on the plug's lip slightly to the left. Check how the plug swims by pulling it alongside the boat. Keep adjusting the eye-screw until your crankbait wobbles in a tight track. Be sure to recheck crankbaits after playing a bass or hanging up. A fish's jaw pressure or excessive line tension can move the eye-screw.

Another important tip is to use a duo-lock style snap or a split ring on the eyes of your crankbaits. Not only do snaps and split rings make knots easier to tie, they allow plugs to work freely, away from the restrictive pull of a tight line. Due to water pressure and line tension, knots tied directly to eyescrews inhibit a crankbait's maximum possible action.

Beginners can take advantage of the built-in action of crankbaits. While worms, jigs and to a degree spinnerbaits must be manipulated by anglers to impart fish-attracting action, crankbaits simply have to be retrieved to attract bass.

Matching crankbaits to whatever bass foods are present is a key to getting strikes. This spring smallmouth went for a crayfish pattern rattling plug.

Choosing Proper Style, Size and Colors for Conditions

One of your prime considerations for choosing a crankbait is to determine which baitfish are present in your home waters. There are many, I imagine, that might argue with that statement, especially when fishing in off-colored conditions. However, when water visibility is above 3 feet, adding sight to sound, especially matching plug colors to available forage fish, certainly helps convince bass to strike. Today, crankbaits are painted so life-like that you should have little trouble finding a likeness in color and shape.

There are general color patterns a beginner can follow. If your target bass species happens to be smallmouth, a crayfish pattern works 100% of the time, as crayfish make up the largest staple food for smallmouths. Crayfish colors also work well for largemouth, especially early season when bigmouths move into shallows where crayfish are abundant. If there are trout, shad or panfish such as bluegill or perch, having some crankbaits in these colors will certainly garner strikes. What is required is a bit of research on your part to find out which species live in your favorite bass water.

Some knowledgeable bass anglers are successful by sticking with this formula for crankbait colors: on bright days with shallow (4 to 6 feet), clear water, a chrome bodied/black backed plug is the choice; for deeper water (6 to 12 feet), less visibility (3 to 6 feet) or dark days, a gold, yellow or white lure with perhaps a bit of red added and for limited visibility (3 feet or less) and early morning/evening low light try black, chartreuse or hot orange. For top water crankbaits, use colors that enhance silhouette, such as black (the most popular) or white.

There is more to choosing the size of crankbait than the obvious consideration of matching size of baitfish bass are after. There is an old adage surrounding bass plugs: the bigger the lure, the bigger the bass. While using a larger profile crankbait may cut down on numbers of strikes from smaller bass (this may be desired where smaller bass are overly abundant and a nuisance), these larger lures may scare bass, while smaller plugs won't. Bigger plugs are harder to work, as they create greater water resistance. When casting large plugs for several hours, fatigue becomes a factor. On the plus side, bigger crankbaits cast easier and dive deeper. Though you may receive more takes with smaller plugs, they generally do not dive as deep and their lighter body weight makes them difficult to cast over 30 feet with a level-wind reel.

Your second consideration for choosing a plug is picking one that dives to depths that bass are holding. Your crankbait must dive to at least that depth, plus a bit extra. All commercially available crankbaits are marked on the packaging as to which depth they are designed to run.

What it comes down to is experimentation and confidence. If you come across a situation where aggressive bass

Adding scents, either liquid or paste type, improves your chances of fooling bass. Scents may be added to any artificial bass lure.

are chasing and attacking crankbaits, color and size mean little as long as plugs run true and are worked at proper depths.

Because crankbaits pull harder than all other bass lures and the tendencies bass display in really hauling off and smacking them, there is temptation to use heavier pound test lines. While 10 and 12 pound tests are standard for crankbaits, here are suggestions for matching lines with diving plugs. Heavy lines, such as 14 to 20 pound tests are fine if you are fishing shallow (less than 6 feet) and the water is stained or somewhat off-color. Heavier lines are thicker in diameter, causing greater water resistance. When you choose a heavier line two things happen. One, heavier lines somewhat restrict freedom of plug movement and most importantly extra water resistance prevents crankbaits from diving to maximum depths. Thinner lines allow freer plug movement and easier access to deeper water holding areas.

"Kneeling and reeling" allowed bass pro Ron Soden to reach this smallmouth without having to change to a deeper running plug.

Basic Crankbait Techniques

When bass are aggressive, simply casting and retrieving at a moderate speed will get strikes. Unfortunately, however, such times are rare, so the bass angler must vary his techniques to achieve consistency.

Speed of retrieve is important. Most anglers unfamiliar with nuances of plugs automatically assume the faster the retrieve, the deeper the lure dives. Not so. Steady reeling swift enough to impart action to the lure is fast enough. A fast retrieve actually reduces depth due to increased water pressure, not unlike water skiing.

While steady retrieves are standard for crankbaits anglers can improve presentations by varying speeds. After you have made your cast, the plug enters the water (make sure the two sets of treble hooks have not fouled the line) and has dived or sunk to the proper depth, a stop-start hesitation can be deadly. Simply stop reeling for a second or two, then begin again. These speed and vibration variations are similar to those of a wounded baitfish.

Often when bass are targeting baitfish on the surface, a diving style plug worked slowly just under the surface film is deadly.

When imitating crayfish, be sure to make your crankbait scrape bottom during the retrieve. The plug's lip stirs up mud and other small debris, creating an illusion of a crayfish making a hasty retreat. During spawning season when bass are building nests, laying eggs or guarding fry they will violently remove any predator that mistakenly wanders into that territory. A crankbait bounced off bottom to resemble a swimming crayfish, which are quite fond of bass eggs, is possibly the best artificial lure to employ at these times.

When bass hold in semi-deep cover (6 to 12 feet) along weedlines, drop-offs or submerged timber (anything from logs to tiny branches), vibrations produced by crankbaits can draw them out. Cast past the bass holding area and make the plug dive until bottom is reached or the lure is bouncing off structure. Work your crankbaits as close as you can alongside and perhaps even slightly into the cover.

Kneeling and Reeling

There may come a time when tossing crankbaits that your plug of choice is just a few feet short of reaching bass holding depths. Here is where a technique called "kneeling and reeling" comes into play. It's as it sounds; to kneel and reel start by dropping to your knees near the edge of the boat or dock. After you have made your cast, simply shove 3/4 of the rod vertically underwater in front of you, holding the reel even with or just below your knees. This technique allows you to add depth, at least a rod's length, without having to change a productive plug to a larger, deeper running model.

Lipless crankbaits, or top water plugs, are the most thrilling lures for bass fishing. Let's face it, it doesn't matter which species of game fish one pursues—Atlantic salmon, tarpon, steelhead or even bass—the most exciting and gratifying takes come when an enraged fish slashes through the surface, pouncing on a lure. When water temperatures are warm (65 to 75 degrees) and bass are feeding in shallow water, top water plugs provide a real thrill.

Top water plugs are normally long and thin in profile. The classic Zara Spook is a well-known and most popular "stick bait". When fished, they are cast as close as possible to bass holding structure and allowed to lay motionless for a tick or two. Holding the rod pointed down at a 4 o'clock position, begin to "twitch" the lure with quick, short wrist-snaps. This causes the top water plug to dart side-to-side. Vary actions and retrieve speeds, sometimes bass prefer a quick twitch and retrieve, other times they may strike the lure as it floats perfectly still. Top waters work best on glass-smooth surfaces, but also work in areas where the surface is so choked with weeds there are no open spots to be seen. Twitching a lipless crankbait on top of thick growth can tease bass to plow right through it and smack the lure. Lipless top water plugs, like all crankbaits, are anything but boring.

Jigs

A "jig" is the name given to a myriad of styles of bass baits with one thing in common: a lead head molded around a hook. From this lead head/hook we can hang a number of plastic/rubber configurations that qualify as jigs. Rubber skirts, pork rinds, tube/skirt baits, sections of or whole plastic worms or marabou, they all fall into the jig category. Jigs can represent a number of prey to bass, most noticeably the crayfish. They are normally used in heavy cover or during cold water periods.

Jigs are popular because they are easy to use, therefore learning how to fish a jig can be somewhat simpler than other bass techniques. They are easy to fish because little action needs to be imparted to them to make them effective. The rule of thumb is to let the cover you happen to be fishing at the time dictate the jig's action. As you work your jig over, around or deflect it off obstructions, these actions alone move it adequately to draw strikes. Their diverse

Examples of correct style lead jig heads for use with grubs and Gitzits. The two on the right are weedless style.

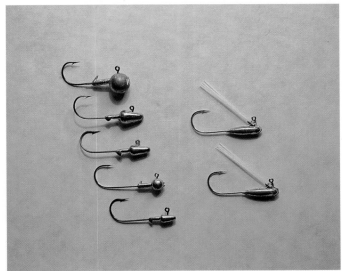

shapes, weights, colors and sizes make jigs ideal for matching water and cover conditions.

Lead head jigs come in many sizes, ranging from as small as 1/32 of an ounce to 5 ounces, however, for most situations 1/4 to 2 ounce heads will be adequate. Heads come in different shapes: round, oval, bullet-shaped or flat. Each has a function. Round or bullet-head jigs sink quickly while flat-head jigs resist water and therefore sink slowly. Round-head jigs can be worked easier through heavy cover without snagging, while bullet-heads are desired around rocky points or bluffs where this shape allows the jig to slip over rock. Because they sink slowly, flat-headed jigs are ideal for shallow water.

Some jigs come with built in stiff plastic weedguards, however, even without the weedguard, jigs are almost snag-free due to the hook riding in the "up" position 90% of the time it is being fished.

Some examples of skirted jigs. These style jigs are excellent in cold water or when worked through very heavy cover.

How to Fish the Jig

Jigs are excellent choices when flipping or pitching. Jigs are fished for bass with three variances in technique: First, perhaps the most popular method of jigging is to work it vertically, that is positioning yourself either above or very close to your target water and by raising and lowering the rod tip the jig is worked straight up and down. When jigging vertically like this in cover, such as grass, treetops or holes in thick vegetation, use a jig weighing 1/2, 5/8 or even 1 ounce. Heavier heads penetrate weeds easier and give you more feel. Begin fishing vertically by allowing the jig to sink straight down until bottom is reached. After it has settled for a second or two, lift the rod tip swiftly to make the jig "leap". Do not reel up, instead allow the jig to fall back on bottom and repeat.

Secondly, the jig can be worked close to the bottom and worked back to the angler in short hops. "Bottom-hopping" is done by casting into the target water and allowing it to sink to bottom, then by reeling in all slack lift the rod tip approximately one foot, then allow the jig to settle, reel in a few feet and repeat. Rock points or sloped banks are ideal for bottom-hopping a jig.

Third, the jig can be simply cast out and retrieved at a steady pace slightly above bottom or structure. This technique works well when bass are holding over a flat area. When retrieving the jig like this it's important to keep it just above the bottom and not have it touch. Dragging jigs along bottom does not represent anything to bass because jigs have no built-in action to them, and dragging them along is quite unnatural. If on your initial cast toward your target water the jig is bumping bottom on the retrieve, reel a bit faster to keep it off the bottom.

When jigging vertically strikes occur primarily on the initial drop after the lure is worked next to cover. If no strike materializes after the first drop raise the jig and allow it to fall again. Because bass hit jigs as they fall it becomes important for the angler to do two things. One, you must keep the line tight at all times. By doing this you are always able to set the hook. Two, you have to control the speed of the free-fall. This is done by using a heavy enough jig head to offset the buoyancy and water resistance created by jig bodies and lines. How heavy a jig head to use is determined once you become familiar with your target water.

Keep in mind there are no set rules for fishing jigs. Speed of retrieve, technique or type of water only gives the angler a starting point. Bass may want something different, so it pays to experiment.

The "jig and pig": jig fitted with a pork trailer. Most bass pros nationwide agree that this lure is the very best for consistently finding the biggest bass.

Jig and Pork Trailer

Better known as the "jig and pig", the addition of a frog-shaped pork rind to a jig has been catching bass for over 50 years, and if nationwide sales are any indicator, jigs and pork trailers will be fooling bass well into the next century. For pitching or flipping there is no better bait.

There are qualities of the pork rind trailer that cannot be ignored. For one, there are few anglers willing to argue the bait's prowess on large bass. Bass fishermen agree on few topics, however, none will deny that a jig and pork frog catches larger bass any time, anywhere, than all other artificial baits. Besides attracting the big boys, the jig and pork trailer is the best choice when water temperatures drop below 60 degrees and, along with split shotting 4 inch worms, seems to always find fish when nothing else in the tackle box even receives a sniff.

The jig and pig work so well because the combination bears a striking resemblance to a crayfish when worked slowly on the bottom. But don't get the impression that this is a slow bait, nor that it is only effective when presented near bottom. While the jig and pork cannot cover as much water in a short time as spinnerbaits and crankbaits, it is fished a bit faster and has a greater attraction radius than plastic worms or smaller jigs. It can also be worked effectively over submerged brush and timber, over and alongside rock points and drop-offs. Pork trailers are more buoyant than plastic baits, therefore they sink slower and can be worked over structure easier.

Pork trailer colors can be important. While the trademark frog pattern may be the first image conjured up whenever pork rind trailers are mentioned they are not the most effective. Black trailers are number one by a long shot, followed by dark brown or either black or brown with some orange or red added.

Basic black and crayfish-colored pork trailers are the two best choices for all-around conditions.

There are a few things you can do to spice up your pork rind trailers to make them even more effective and appealing to bass. Pork rind baits are high maintenance, that is they have to be kept moist when out of the water or they become "crispy" and lose their supple action. Pork rinds hold scents well so add scent oils to the jar of rinds before use. Also, some anglers add a few drops of glycerine (available at drug stores) to each jar. Doing this makes the pork softer which translates to more action imparted to the jig, also, bass will hold onto the lure longer.

Here is a great tip to make the jig and pig more effective. Thread a 1/4 to 1/2 inch section of plastic worm head onto the bend of the hook before you add the pork trailer. By doing this the pork cannot slip down towards the jig body, keeping the jig in correct balance and forcing the pork to stay in perfect position on the bottom of the hook bend.

Some examples of grubs. These baits are a favorite of smallmouth fishermen.

Grubs

The grub is a variation of a jig, and is essentially a round, worm-like stubby soft plastic body with a short tail. Legendary lure maker and expert angler Tom Mann brought the small plastic grub from the saltwater angler's tackle box into the public eye in 1960. Even though grubs proved to be an excellent bass bait, it wasn't until the early 1970s that grubs became popular with professionals. Bass anglers in Washington state find that grubs produce somewhat larger fish than traditional split shotting techniques.

The best sizes for "grubbing" are 1 to 3 inch bodied lures, however, the 2-inch grub is more popular and productive for bass fishing. Grubs come with basically two types of tails: straight, or "stubby" that impart little action, or the "swimming tail" version that features a long, thin, curved flat tail that undulates seductively when worked even at a slow retrieve. The curly-tailed grub is by far the most popular and versatile.

Since grubs are classified as jigs they work best when rigged with 1/8, 1/4 and 1/2 ounce lead heads on long-shanked #1/0 and #2/0 hooks. Since the thick head of a grub makes Texas rigging impractical and most grubbing is done over areas where there is little chance for snags, the hook is rigged exposed near the narrow spot where the tail meets body. When rigging the grub be sure to follow the "seam" on the lure body when threading in the hook. This ensures the tail will hang either up or down and keep the grub at an even keel, swimming straight and appearing more natural.

There are possibly dozens of different techniques and types of holding areas where grubs are effective, however there are several that are most commonly employed.

The first and most popular method for grubs is to find slopes, drop-offs or rip-rap banks in 10 to 15 feet of water. Position yourself at a workable casting distance straight out from the target area. Cast toward shore and allow the grub to sink on a tight line. Begin retrieving in short jigs, allowing the grub to sink back toward bottom between hops. Present the grub so it stays 12 to 18 inches off bottom during the retrieve. It frequently pays to allow the grub to lay still on bottom for a few extra seconds before starting another hopping sequence. Many times a curious bass will suck in the lure as it lays motionless.

The second way to work a grub is the easiest. Choose a curly-tailed grub and simply cast toward the target water. Allow the lure to sink to bottom or proper depth and begin a steady retrieve. Do not move or twitch the rod tip, merely hold it steady at a 10 o'clock position and slowly wind the reel. The rippling action of the tail is all that is necessary to get old bucketmouth's attention.

When fishing steep drop-offs it may pay to fish the grub parallel to the shoreline. Not only is it easier to keep grubs near bottom on steep drop-offs, you are presenting the grub in the most productive depth for longer periods. By staying parallel you can fish grubs much shallower and use lighter jig heads for a slower presentation.

Grubs can be split shotted much the same as 4 inch worms. Place a small shot 18 to 24 inches up the line above the grub and present it the same way you would a worm.

Curly-tail grubs are one of the best baits for suspended bass. If you suspect bass are hovering over a submerged hump or tree, try dead-drifting grubs with the wind (or if fishing in dead-calm conditions, troll them very slowly with your electric motor) over the area. The movement of the waves and current is enough to trigger strikes. Though strikes on grubs are usually firm and easy to detect, pay close attention when grubbing as about half the time a bass simply sips them in, causing a tiny "thump" or a change in line direction.

Best colors for grubs are similar to those you would choose for worms under similar conditions. Local professionals prefer smoke, brown/black flake, black/metal flake, green/metal flake, white and motor oil.

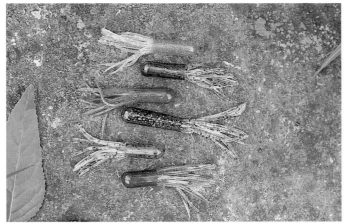

Some examples of Gitzits. These baits are a favorite of smallmouth fishermen.

Gitzits

Gitzit is an odd name for such a wonderful plastic bait. They are also called "finesse baits" (or unlovingly "sissy baits") because hooking fish with these small lures requires a higher degree of sensitivity and presentation skill than other methods. The Gitzit, a tube-shaped, hollow-bodied jig with squid-like tentacles on one end, has been a popular plastic bait in Western bass waters since the early 1980s, and is just now becoming popular elsewhere.

Gitzits work best in situations where bass have been fished hard or in open, clear water. Like all jig fishing they are most effective on the drop and that is when you get the majority of takes. Gitzits sink at a 45 degree angle and fall rather swiftly, therefore the best way to work a Gitzit is to fish it as slowly as possible and stay as close to the target area as you can. The Gitzit is a tiny, light jig and after you have more than 25 feet of line out it becomes difficult to control the action. There are three situations where Gitzits shine.

The first and most celebrated technique for Gitzits is a technique called "twitching". Cast toward the target water and allow the Gitzit to sink and retrieve it slowly while giving the rod tip swift, short wrist-snaps.

The second popular technique when fishing Gitzits, especially out West, is skipping them under docks. The compact shape and weight of the Gitzit makes it skip easier than most artificial baits. After the Gitzit is skipped under the dock do not give it any additional action, simply allow it to sink to bottom. Bass will strike it on the downfall.

"Twitching" is the best technique for fishing Gitzits. This 3 pounder found a twitched tube good enough to eat.

The most important thing to remember when fishing the Gitzit is to have enough slack in your line to allow the lure to fall, but not so much that you cannot feel a subtle take. Most bites will be soft, so much so that an angler's only clue a bass has sipped it in is a slight movement of line or a soft resistance.

When finesse fishing with Gitzits, you will be using light lines from 4 to 8 pound test, 6 being the most popular and effective. Lighter lines allow lures to work more naturally and you will receive more strikes.

Gitzits are a tiny bait, bodies range from 3/4 to 4 inches long; 2-1/2 to 3 inch baits are best. With these small bodies you have to match them with proper sized jig heads and fine wire hooks. Lead jig heads in 1/32, 1/16 and 1/4 ounce are best, built with #1/0 and #2/0 fine wire hooks. Don't be deceived here, these jig hooks may be labeled "1/0" or "2/0", but actually they are much smaller, they appear to be closer to #1 or #1/0.

Two examples of properly rigged jigs: a Gitzit (top) and a grub (bottom).

Chapter 5

The Tools:
Rods, Reels and Lines

Now that we know how to find bass, have learned some techniques and can choose an artificial bait, we now have to consider casting equipment options: rods, reels and lines. Selecting complimentary gear components is nearly as important as being able to find bass and choosing a technique to match conditions.

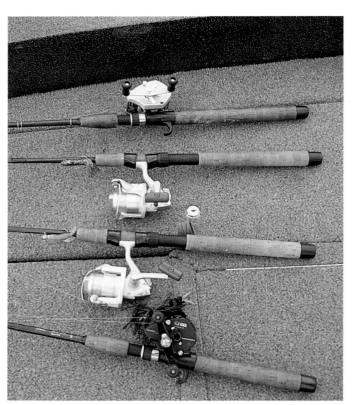

The tools for bass fishermen: a collection of high quality rods, reels and lines to take on any challenging condition.

Rods: The Important Match

Just as a professional bowler would not bring one ball to a tournament, nor a touring golfer just a couple clubs, bass anglers must have enough rods in their arsenal to effectively execute all techniques.

Your first consideration when purchasing a bass rod is to get the highest quality graphite composite you can afford. While it is true that skill lands many more bass

than equipment, it's the extra sensitivity of premium quality rods that allows you to feel the lightest biters, permits you to feel exactly how a lure is working (such as revolutions of a spinner blade, the wobble of a crankbait or the slight bumping of a worm on bottom) and lightweight graphite blanks do not promote fatigue after hours of casting.

Today's bass rods are built to accommodate either spinning or level-wind (baitcasting) reels. For spinning rods you have a myriad of choices for practical handle designs, what it boils down to is which one feels comfortable in your hands. For level-wind reels, I would highly recommend any model with a trigger style handle. Triggers give bass fishermen three major advantages: 1) They are usually built in direct contact with the rod blank, adding extra feel. 2) On cold days triggers allow for an easier grip on the rod. 3) Playing fish and, unfortunately, breaking off when snagged is done without having to squeeze the rod handle.

Bass rods are available with three built-in "actions", that determine where and how the rod will flex. There are fast, medium and slow action bass rods. Fast action means the greatest amount of flex is in the top quarter of the blank; medium action means the blank flexes in the top half and in a slow action rod the blank flexes uniformly through the top three-quarters. These three actions determine how heavy a lure or weight or pound test line will match as well as how much power the rod has (in terms of setting the hook and how much force can be put on a played fish). All commercially manufactured rods have a suggested lure weight/pound test line recommendation on the base of the blank near the handle.

Always purchase rods that have the correct number of guides. An easy rule to follow when buying a rod is one guide for each foot of rod. For example, a 7 foot rod should have no fewer than 7 guides, counting the tip. Remember, it's the rod that fights a bass, not the line. When there are too few guides the line follows the rod contour unevenly causing stress points on the line. There must be enough guides so that the line follows the bend of the rod as closely as possible. This is most important when using lighter lines. Look for rods with guides that protect lines from abrasion, made of either ceramic, hardaloy or SIC, which have the least amount of friction and are the highest quality. Unlike plain metal guides that eventually wear into a groove and cause line damage, these guides can withstand years of constant use and show zero wear.

When selecting a rod you have to factor in several variables to determine your choices. How heavy a lure will you be casting? You want a rod that won't over-flex from too heavy a lure, yet will flex enough to propel a cast when using light lures. What pound test line will you be using? You want a rod that protects light lines, although on the flip side when using heavy lines a stouter rod with minimal flex is the choice. Will you be fishing in heavy cover or over wide open areas? Are the bass you expect to catch pan sized or do you anticipate bucketmouths in the double-digit category? All these variables have to be taken into consideration before you make a cast.

If you examine rod racks of touring pro bassers you will find anywhere from 6 to 10 different rods in various lengths and actions. However, for the beginner, there are three basic rod lengths/actions that adequately cover the bases.

The first is a medium action, 6 to 6-1/2 foot spinning rod rated for 6 to 10 or 6 to 12 pound line and 1/8th to 3/8th ounce lures. This rod will be your standard for smaller artificials, such as Gitzits, grubs, 4 inch worms for split shotting and other similar sized baits. This is a great rod for fishing open water.

The second is a medium action 6 to 6-1/2 foot spinning or baitcasting rod rated for 8 to 12 or 8 to 17 pound line and 3/8th to 3/4 ounce lures. This rod is ideal for crankbaits and spinnerbaits and qualifies as an "all-purpose" bass stick. There isn't any technique you can't practice efficiently with this weight rod.

The third rod for beginners is a baitcasting outfit, a fast action, 6 foot rod rated for 10 to 20 pound line and 1/4 to 1 ounce lures. A strong blank like this is perfect for pitching and flipping, ideal for large jigs, larger plastic worms and Slug-Gos. This is the rod to choose when casting into thick cover, where you have to turn bass away from obstructions immediately.

When I fish tiny jigs, Gitzits, grubs or when split shotting, I use a rod that is just a bit unorthodox but still produces great results. My slow action spinning rod is 9-1/2 feet, rated for 4 to 8 pound line. When split shotting, not only can I get much longer sweeps when slowly presenting a 4 inch worm (therefore keeping the worm moving for longer periods than a shorter rod), the light action blank really hoops over making even the smallest bass an interesting battle. It's a marvelous "sissy bait" rod.

Whichever rod manufacturer or blank composites you choose keep in mind that these three rods are the most common and popular with bass fishermen nationwide because they can cover just about any situation and technique. They are the perfect foundation for a bass rod collection.

Reels: A Matter of Choice

Technology has come a long way since the early days of bass fishing. About the time my father was born my grand-dad bought a state-of-the-art bass reel, the direct drive Pflueger Supreme, a.k.a. The Thumb Burner Special. While my grandfather was proud of his new reel, and he sure caught plenty of bass with it, today's reels are nothing short of miraculous in comparison. Backlashes were sometimes the norm with the old crude level-winds, but reels that grace sporting goods shelves are now so well made and simple to operate that their use is but an afterthought.

Although you may occasionally still see some Pflueger Supremes in use, there are two types of reels in popular use today: level wind (baitcasting) and spinning. Closed-face reels have not found a place in the bass fisherman's heart, possibly due to poor line capacity or inferior drag systems.

Bass anglers have two choices for reels, the baitcasting, or level wind reel or . . .

. . . the more popular spinning style reel.

periods; they can be cast effectively from any position and no matter how much the wind slows a cast, there is no fear of backlash.

Beginners unskilled with baitcasting reels can do themselves a favor by learning with spinning reels before dealing with inevitable backlashes. Spinning reels are almost foul proof.

When choosing a spinning reel there are two types of drag systems: rear and spool top. Rear drags are easier to get at when playing a hot fish, however it's often difficult to remember which way to turn the knob. You have to momentarily look away from your rod and bolting fish to either loosen or tighten the drag. Spool top drags are easier to operate, but you have to reach around your line to adjust tension.

Level winds may take a bit more practice and thought to use, but they have advantages. Baitcasting reels have superior drag systems due to line coming off the spool in a straight line instead of a 90 degree angle off the bail of a spinning reel, which increases friction and creates a weak point in the line. Level winds are best used with larger, heavier lures; these reels require more weight to pull line from the spool when casting—crankbaits are always used with level wind reels for this reason, not only because of the weight of the plugs but also the pull or resistance they create when worked through water. Heavy jigs and larger spinnerbaits are also used with baitcasting reels. More power can be exerted with level winds because you can use your thumb along with the drag system to really sock it to a bass on the hookset, or use the added force to turn large fish away from obstructions.

Spinning reels are definitely the choice when casting small, light lures, such as grubs, Gitzits, tiny Slug-Gos or when split shotting 4 inch worms. Line pays off a spinning reel spool effortlessly because unlike a baitcasting reel the spool does not revolve. Techniques like skipping are best done with spinning reels, due to the extreme variations of speed that line is payed off the spool and so abruptly stopped—a level-wind would surely be engulfed in a huge birds-nest unless you happen to have a very educated thumb.

Spinning reels work best with lighter lines, 6, 8 and 10 pound test, due to heavier monofilaments having more "memory" and a tendency to leap off the spool in coils. When line does this it makes casting, or trying to cast for any distance, difficult. Spinning reels are also a good choice whenever fishing in tight quarters or during windy

Here is a great tip to make your level wind reel cast farther and work smoother. Start by carefully taking your reel apart, specifically all moving parts (gears, drag system, etc.) and clean all grease and oil. Use toothpaste and a stiff toothbrush for the job. (Colgate works best.) Toothpaste is a mild abrasive that will thoroughly clean all moving parts to the bare metal. Get a cotton swab, dip it in Slick 50 Oil Treatment and apply a thin coat to all moving parts of the reel. The result is a reel that casts farther and works exceptionally smooth. Grease, even though it is a lubricant, is thick in comparison and can hinder a reel's performance in colder weather.

Unlike spinning reels, baitcasting reels can keep you in contact with bottom longer and easier. Line can be fed with ease by disengaging the spool or leaving it in the free-spool position and allowing line to slip off the reel by "feathering" the spool with your thumb. Level winds work best with heavier lines, 10 pound test and up, because the thicker lines have less tendency to backlash.

Look for simplicity when choosing a reel. Many extras such as speed-changing gears and drag adjustments are really nothing more than gimmicks and do little to actually improve a reel's performance. Your reels should have at least medium capacity spools, capable of holding at least 100 yards of line. Also, look for reels with high gear ratios, such as 4.5:1, 5.2:1 and 5.6:1. Higher gear ratios allow you to catch up with a bass that has picked up a lure or bait and is moving rapidly towards you, and most importantly, faster line retrieval means more time presenting and less time reeling between casts.

Regardless of which type of reel you choose, purchase the highest quality you can afford. Butter-smooth drags, non-wobbling, easily turned handles and a general solid feeling are all things to look for. Brand names like Shimano, Ryobi, Daiwa, Garcia, Penn, Ambassadeur and Quantum all can't-miss when it comes to quality.

Lines: The Critical Connection

Possibly the single most important date in sportfishing history was the patent of monofilament lines by DuPont in 1938. Even though at the time the nylon synthetic fiber was sold by the company to other manufacturers for use in braided lines and fly lines, it was the beginning of a revolution. With the explosion of sportfishing in the early 1950s, mostly due to the invention of the spinning reel, came the demand for more castable lines. When DuPont introduced Stren (1957) and Berkley introduced Dew Flex (1958), these new monofilaments changed sportfishing like no other previous event.

Bass fishermen have access to the best quality lines ever produced. Improvements in chemical and extruder technology have produced lines that are far better than monofilaments were when Eisenhower was in the Oval Office. There are a dozen or more premium monos available today, but regardless which brand you choose, keep one thought in mind: always buy the highest quality line you can afford. High quality lines are more expensive for good reason. They are stronger and last a lot longer. Saving a few pennies on a lower grade line does not lessen the anguish of a lost trophy.

Today's lines are thinner, have tremendous tensile strength, greater flexibility, greater knot strength and less memory. They

are available in colors ranging from fluorescent blue, green and gold to subtle tone browns, greens, pinks and clear. Which monos are right for the bass fisherman? Following are characteristics to look for.

First, your line has to be premium quality with high tensile strength which means superior knot strength and high abrasion resistance. These are the two most important features to look for in a line. Your knots must be able to withstand the shock of strikes, hooksets and bolting fish, and due to the nature of bass fishing—casting and playing fish around submerged trees and rocks—an abrasion resistant line is necessary.

Limpness is a significant characteristic in a bass line. Limp lines are more easily cast, perform better in cold weather and most importantly, allow finesse baits (Gitzits, Slug-Gos, grubs and small jigs) and especially worms to work naturally, unhindered by stiff lines. Light-biting or wary bass cannot feel a limp line as easily as a stiff one, therefore they are likely to hold onto baits a bit longer. Do keep in mind that limp lines have a bit more stretch than stiffer monofilaments.

Use a line that can be followed visually. Natural colored lines are nearly impossible to follow during a presentation. When using monos that disappear into the glare, you are handicapping yourself by not knowing if you have worked the same area twice, you do not know if your bait is working too close or too far away from an obstruction and most importantly many strikes are not felt in the rod but rather seen by a twitching or slight movement of the line. By using a visible line you can work your bait closer to obstructions without guesswork and detect light pick-ups.

The best colors for a visible line range from fluorescent colors for dark days or when there is some color to the water, to clear or pink lines when conditions are bright with unlimited visibility. Fluorescent blues and clear lines seem to be the best all-around colors for bass fishing. You may still use a bright fluorescent line in clear water or on

There are approximately a dozen premium quality monofilaments the bass angler can choose from. Get the best you can afford.

bright days without tipping off bass by coloring the first few feet of line above your lure with a black, waterproof marking pen. Running the marker up and down the line a few times camouflages the fluorescent color.

No matter which color or brand of line you choose, be sure to replace it often, after approximately 2 or 3 trips, depending on use. Abrasion, line twist, playing fish and breaking off on snags stretches and weakens lines, even the best ones. Purchasing lines in bulk spools not only saves money but allows you to change to fresh line often. There is no need to empty a spool each time you change line; 80 to 100 yards of mainline is all that is required. Only changing this much line will save money, besides, a any bass that can peel off this much line has yet to be hooked on earth. Fill your reel 1/4 to 1/2 full of braided nylon backing before spooling on the mainline. Braided nylon is an excellent choice for backing, as it is much stronger than the mainline and will last years before it needs replacing.

Know your brand of line's capacity. Lines can vary greatly in their actual pound test between brands. Don't assume that just because a line is labeled "10 pound test" that it breaks after 10 pounds of pressure is exerted. For example, some 10 pound test lines actually break at 16. Lines labeled as "IGFA" or "Line Class" are very close to their advertised break strength. Again, be familiar with your brand.

Be sure to regularly check your line for abrasion and nicks. Run your thumb and forefinger along the section you have been using, usually the first 40 yards or so. If it feels rough, clip it off. Nicked, rough line greatly lowers the pound test and knot strength. Also, keep your reels and line spools out of hot car trunks and direct sunlight. Rods hanging in the back of a pickup might look stylish, but heat and UV rays damage monofilament. The best place to store lines and reels is always cool and dark.

There is a new wave of lines on the market, the ultra strong, ultra thin lines made from Spectra and Kevlar fibers. These lines, available in such colors as white, black and dull yellow, test from 30 to 70 pound test yet have the diameter of 8 and 12 pound lines. At first inspection, an angler might think he has stumbled upon the greatest line available. However, these seemingly unbeatable lines have some very serious flaws. Unlike monofilament lines, these new wave lines do not stretch, which can be an advantage setting the hook, but think about what happens to your rod. Most rods, especially high modulus composite (read "fragile") component rods, cannot accommodate these non-stretching lines with any more pressure than a regular hook-set. Exploding rods are all too frequent when these lines are used and it is common practice by all major rod companies to void warranties when rods are broken by these unforgiving lines. Even though these lines are incredibly strong, only lines made from Kevlar fibers have any abrasion resistance. Spectra fibers are incredibly fragile; if your line even brushes against a log or rock, they abraid and snap as easily as cotton thread. Regular knots will not hold together with these lines, you must use knots recommended by manufacturers or use a super-glue type adhesive to keep them from unravelling. As far as beginning bass fishermen are concerned, stick with the tried and true quality monofilaments and Don't mess with these high-tech fiber lines. 🐟

Knots

Improved Clinch Knot

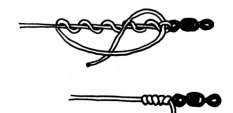

Trilene Knot

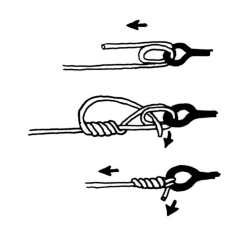

Palomar Knot

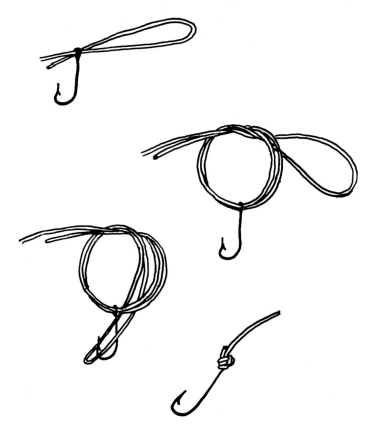

A WORD ON CATCH AND RELEASE

Lee Wulff, one of the most famous outdoor authors and fly fishermen, coined a phrase many years ago that rings even truer today: "A game fish is much too valuable to be caught only once." Although Lee was talking primarily about Atlantic salmon, bass anglers can also take a leaf from his book of ethics.

There is no question that most bass fishermen release a good portion, if not all, of their catch. Much of this attitude comes from high-profile professional tournament anglers who practice nothing but catch and release. With the tremendous popularity of bass fishing in America and the number of anglers growing exponentially each year, practicing catch and release assures quality angling opportunities for the future.

Although some lakes and reservoirs can benefit from keeping bass (due to overpopulations and stunted fish), as a general rule an angler can do nothing but improve a fishery by releasing his catch. Here are tips that will aid you in playing and releasing bass unharmed.

1) Play bass as quickly as possible to avoid exhausting the fish. This reduces shock and lactic acid buildup in the muscle tissue which may result in death.

2) When landing bass, avoid using a landing net—the netting rubs off the fish's protective slime coat. Bring the fish alongside the boat or shore and grasp it firmly by the lower lip. Keep fingers out of the gills; if a gill is ruptured the fish will bleed and possibly die. Grasping the bass by the lower lip temporarily paralyzes the fish, allowing you to remove the hook while it stays relatively still.

3) If a bass is deeply hooked in the throat or in the gills do not attempt to remove the hook but instead cut the line as close to the hook as you can. Naturally produced acids eventually dissolve hooks.

4) Most of the time a bass correctly released will swim immediately away. If it lays on its side or appears disoriented, grasp the fish just above the tail and work it back and forth gently until it regains its strength. When it starts to struggle it is fully revived. Release the tail and let it go to fight another day.

Good fishing, and I'll see you on the lake.

LEARN MORE ABOUT FLY FISHING AND FLY TYING WITH THESE BOOKS

If you are unable to find the books shown below at your local book store
or fly shop you can order direct from the publisher below.

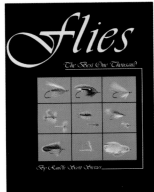

Flies: The Best One Thousand
Randy Stetzer
$24.95

Fly Tying Made Clear and Simple
Skip Morris
$19.95 (HB: $29.95)

The Art of Tying the Dry Fly
Skip Morris
$29.95 (HB:$39.95)

Curtis Creek Manifesto
Sheridan Anderson
$7.95

American Fly Tying Manual
Dave Hughes
$9.95

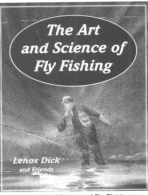

The Art and Science of Fly Fishing
Lenox Dick
$19.95

Western Hatches
Dave Hughes, Rick Hafele
$24.95

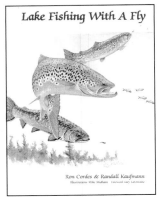

Lake Fishing with a Fly
Ron Cordes, Randall Kaufmann
$26.95

Advanced Fly Fishing for Steelhead
Deke Meyer
$24.95

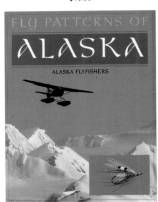

Fly Patterns of Alaska
Alaska Flyfishers
$19.95

Fly Tying & Fishing for Panfish and Bass
Tom Keith
$19.95

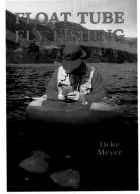

Float Tube Fly Fishing
Deke Meyer
$11.95

VISA, MASTERCARD or AMERICAN EXPRESS ORDERS CALL TOLL FREE: 1-800-541-9498
(9-5 Pacific Standard Time)

Or Send Check or money order to:

Frank Amato Publications
Box 82112
Portland, Oregon 97282

(Please add $3.00 for shipping and handling)

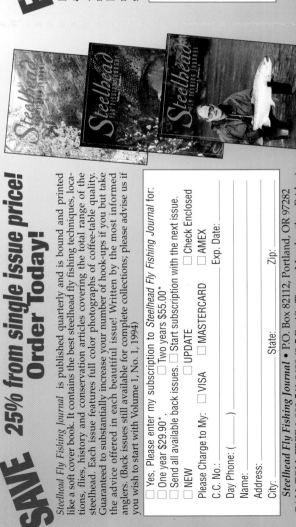